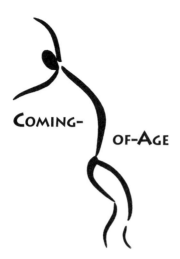

COMING-
OF-AGE

COMING-
OF-AGE

**TRADITIONS
AND RITUALS
AROUND
THE WORLD**

KAREN LIPTAK

*The Millbrook Press
Brookfield, Connecticut*

Editorial Consultant: Beth Steinhorn,
Anthropology Educator, Denver Museum of Natural History

Published by The Millbrook Press
2 Old New Milford Road, Brookfield, Connecticut 06804

Photographs courtesy of Photo Researchers: pp. 11 (© Susan Szasz), 14
(© Hubertus Kanus), 57 (© George Holton), 81 (© Eugene Gordon), 92
(© Porterfield/Chickering); Anthro-Photo: pp. 25 (Napoleon A. Chagnon),
36 (Majoree Shostal), 45 (Mark R. Jenike), 50 (Stuart Smucker), 86
(M. Nichter); © National Geographic Society: pp. 30, 33 (Harald
Schultz), 68 (Bill Hess); © Monty Roessel: p. 72; Japan National
Tourist Organization: p. 101; Brandon Hammond: p. 107.

Library of Congress Cataloging-in-Publication Data
Liptak, Karen.
Coming-of-age : traditions and rituals around the world / by Karen Liptak.
p.   cm.
Includes bibliographical references and index.
ISBN 1-56294-243-3 (lib. bdg.)
1. Puberty rites—Cross-cultural studies—Juvenile literature.
2. Adolescence—Cross-cultural studies—Juvenile literature.   I. Title.
GN483.3.L57   1994   392'.14—dc20   93-1414   CIP   AC

CONTENTS

COMING-
OF-AGE

CHAPTER ONE

GROWING UP HUMAN

During childhood, we depend upon our parents for our needs. As adults, we are expected to be responsible members of society capable of raising children of our own. Between childhood and adulthood we all go through a period of astounding transformation. It is a time of great physical, intellectual, emotional, social, and spiritual change. It is called adolescence.

The concept of adolescence and the way it is acknowledged are by no means universal. Each society defines adolescence according to its needs.

In societies of hunter-gatherers, in which hunting animals and gathering plants is the means of subsistence, adolescence is often relatively short, if it exists at all. These societies are usually divided into small bands organized around the constant need to search for food. Each person's contribution to the band is of vital importance to its survival. Children generally grow up to take over the roles of their parents, and the sooner each member of the band accepts adult responsibilities, the better for the group.

In agricultural societies people tend to settle in one place and raise crops to survive. The entire group needs to work in the fields. Here, too, the needs of the society are best served by a relatively short adolescence.

In industrialized societies, the need for years of schooling and training for jobs has resulted in a prolonged period of transition between childhood and adulthood. [1]

Although many of us who live in industrialized societies agree that adolescence is a special stage of life, its characteristics vary. These include the age at which it begins and how long it lasts. Adolescence can span any number of years between the ages of eight and twenty-one. The period itself can be filled with turmoil, or it can be smooth, as it reportedly is in Samoa and other South Pacific island societies.

The way adolescents view themselves depends upon the way society views them. This picture will always be subject to change. However, there is one unifying element in the experience of adolescents around the world, and that is the physical transformation known as puberty.

All adolescents go through puberty. During this time, the body becomes ready to reproduce. Some of

AMERICAN GIRLS DANCE AT HOME. AS MEMBERS OF AN INDUSTRIALIZED COUNTRY, THEY ARE IN THE MIDST OF THE LENGTHY PERIOD OF PHYSICAL AND EMOTIONAL GROWTH KNOWN AS ADOLESCENCE.

the changes, such as a spurt of growth in height and weight, are shared by boys and girls. Other changes are unique to one sex. And the pace of puberty varies in any two people, whether they are of the same sex or not.

On the average, girls reach puberty at an earlier age than boys; girls may start showing physical changes at age eight, while boys won't begin until age ten or older. The healthier and better nourished people are, the earlier puberty reportedly occurs. Stress and climate may also play a part.[2] In the United States and most of Western Europe today, the average age of puberty is between twelve and thirteen years for girls and fourteen years for boys.

The most noticeable sign of puberty for females is the menarche, or the start of menstruation. Each month when a woman of childbearing age is not pregnant, she will appear to bleed from the vagina, usually for a few days. Although the exact moment when a boy is said to come of age may vary, a girl's coming-of-age is easily identified as the menarche.

COMING-OF-AGE · In most societies, it is traditional to give both boys and girls new duties, knowledge, and rights when they reach adolescence to prepare them to become adults. In many groups, adolescents also receive increased spiritual education, and they are told secrets that are concealed from children (and perhaps from the other sex as well). This new knowledge, and the new social status accompanying it, is often marked by ritual.

This book is about these special coming-of-age rituals, which are initiations in a ceremonial form.

Rituals give children—known as initiates—a new adult identity in their group. They help to protect the initiates and prepare them for the future, as well as to emphasize the importance of the event for both the individual and the group. Finally, they herald the future contributions initiates will be expected to make to their society.

Not all societies hold coming-of-age rituals, but where they do take place, they are generally performed around the age of puberty.[3] Some anthropologists link the observance of coming-of-age ceremonies to the structure of a society.

Ceremonies held for girls are most commonly found in hunter-gatherer societies. Researchers suggest that because these societies are divided into small bands, women of childbearing age are crucial for their contribution to subsistence as well as for their value in producing new members of the band. Coming-of-age ceremonies for females are considered a way to protect them and to assure their reproductive capability and general competence.[4]

Ceremonies for boys are frequent in Africa and South America and in agricultural societies throughout the world. These ceremonies are often held for several boys at once as a way to encourage them to bond with their fellow initiates. In agricultural societies, both sexes are likely to have longer ceremonies than in food-gathering societies. This may be due to the need for strong ties beyond the family to hold these societies together. The men, who are usually the ones running the community, are encouraged to bond together to create a support system for one another. Although the ceremonies are intended to

A MASAI BOY HERDS CATTLE IN TANZANIA. HE WILL UNDERGO
A DRAMATIC COMING-OF-AGE RITUAL THAT WILL TRANSFORM HIM
FROM A CHILD INTO A RESPECTED HUNTER AND WARRIOR.

ensure male as well as female fertility, for boys there is perhaps more focus on bravery and the ability to take on adult duties.[5]

However, when societies are industrialized and the need for many children and male bonding decreases in significance, adolescent initiation ceremonies take different forms. Rituals are replaced by other types of social markers. These are mostly legal milestones, such as obtaining a driver's license, registering to vote, reaching the legal drinking age, or being old enough to join the military.

Many anthropologists consider contemporary religious ceremonies as coming-of-age rituals because they initiate an individual into full adult standing in his or her spiritual community.[6] In the United States, such religious ceremonies include Jewish Bar Mitzvahs and Bat Mitzvahs, as well as Christian confirmations.

Wherever and in whatever form coming-of-age ceremonies are held, they mean as much to the community as they do to the individual. Their very existence offers the promise that the group will survive and its traditions be passed on. Since initiates usually go through the same rituals their parents and grandparents did at the same age, a link is formed with the past and between family and community. The impact of these ceremonies is great, yet the reason for their practice is often shrouded in mystery.

COMMON THREADS · The rituals covered in this book show a variety of ways in which young people are initiated into their adult community. Some are for both boys and girls, although most differ for each sex. Some are very elaborate; others are very simple.

Some are extremely brief; others may go on for several months or over a year. Some take place for one person at a time; others are group events. (This is primarily true for males and very common among traditional African cultures.) Most are painless, but some cause physical discomfort or even great pain. Some involve grand feasts, others call for fasts, and still others incorporate both.

Here are some themes common to many coming-of-age rituals:

Symbolic death and rebirth. The initiate dies as a child and is reborn as an adult. Many symbols are incorporated into the ceremonies to support this theme. White face paint may represent death; a mother's involvement may symbolize her giving birth for a second time to her child as an adult; the child may receive a new name, symbolic of being reborn with a new identity; and the initiate may be formally presented to the community as if he or she were a person the others had not known before.

Isolation of the initiate. Because the period between the symbolic death of the child and the rebirth of the adult leaves an individual without an identity, many communities believe the initiate is particularly vulnerable to dangers at this time. In order to protect the "nonperson," he or she is often isolated.

Isolation can also provide an individual with the time to learn the responsibilities, and in some cases the secrets, of being an adult. It is an opportunity for the initiate to reflect on his or her new status and to adjust to the enormous changes, which can be exciting, scary, challenging, and confusing all at once.

Isolating the initiate gives the community time to adjust to the changes as well. By physically removing the child from its presence, the child "dies" in its eyes. When the initiate returns as an adult, the community is ready to accept him or her as a new member of society.

Finally, the initiate (particularly young women during their first menses) may be viewed as dangerously powerful to the society, so isolation can protect the community as well. Some anthropologists believe that in hunter-gatherer societies females during their menses are considered dangerous to men because blood is known to frighten away certain animals. So, contact with female blood may have come to be seen as threatening to a successful hunt.7

In many tribal societies, a female will continue to be isolated from males whenever she menstruates. That first menstruation will differ from future ones, however, because at its onset the young woman is instructed about her future feminine tasks, including etiquette, menstrual observances, and pregnancy taboos. In many societies, a female's initiation is a prelude to marriage, which follows soon after.

Physical changes. Tattoos, scars, or piercings are permanent physical changes that mark an individual as an initiated member of society. These visible signs are often more important for boys than for girls. The menarche is a concrete event that lets a girl know that she is becoming a woman. However, puberty for boys lacks such a dramatic physical sign. Perhaps this is the reason that a male's new social status in many tribes is accompanied by visible body scars.

Circumcision (cutting off the skin that covers the tip of the penis) is the most dramatic body document of a new stage in life. It continues to be held in conjunction with coming-of-age ceremonies in many cultures. (In the United States, circumcisions are traditionally performed shortly after birth for religious or health reasons.) Several cultures also have a circumcision operation for girls.*

Other physical alterations or ornaments serve to identify the initiate only during the ceremony. These include masks, special body paint, elaborate clothes, new hairdos, and jewelry that may protect the initiates or merely help them celebrate the day.

Cleansing. Upon entering or leaving seclusion, many initiates are ritually cleansed. This helps prepare them for receiving a new identity. Cleansing does not only take the form of bathing; there are other symbolic acts of cleansing, such as cutting hair, pouring water, dressing in new clothes, and cleaning the house.

Tests of endurance, bravery, or competence. Primarily with young men, but occasionally among women as well, initiations incorporate physical or emotional tests to help ensure that the initiate is ready for the challenges and responsibilities of adulthood.

Teaching and learning. Most ceremonies include a section during which the youngster is taught by el-

* This operation, usually accompanied by ceremony, involves removing all or most of the external female sex organs. During the least drastic type of female circumcision, known as a clitoridectomy, the tip of the clitoris is cut off. An estimated 100 million women living today in African, Far Eastern, and Middle Eastern countries have been circumcised. This includes nearly all women in Somalia, Ethiopia, and Sudan. The practice has become controversial, however, because it can lead to long-term complications, including serious infections, as well as menstrual, sexual, and fertility problems. According to a 1993 wire service report, the World Health Organization—an agency of the United Nations—says that female circumcision "kills tens of thousands of women and condemns millions to a life of agony." The agency has approved a resolution to call for tougher action against the custom. But much education is needed; in Kenya, for instance, where the tradition has been outlawed since 1982, up to half the women in the country continue to be circumcised.

ders, teachers, parents, or others. Some of the teachings are secrets; others are simply lessons that adults must know. Initiates often establish a kinship with their instructors. If they go through a group initiation, the ties are with their peers as well. At the same time, their learning may sever initiates' ties with others who, either because of their sex or because they have not yet come of age, are barred from learning the secrets.

Community and sharing of food. The communal aspect of the ceremony is essential. Rarely do coming-of-age rituals occur without others there to witness at least a portion of them. The ceremonies are not only for the initiates, but are designed to help the whole society adjust to the initiates' transition from childhood to adulthood.

One common form of community participation is eating together. Many ceremonies incorporate communal food or feasting. Some also relate communal food events to other aspects of the initiation, so that they incorporate a boy sharing his first kill or a girl serving food to the family. Taking these a step further, the sharing of kill or serving of food is a symbol of the values and characteristics that a youngster is expected to have as an adult. Boys should grow to be brave and skillful hunters; girls should grow to be generous and industrious women. The ceremony, then, is the initiate's and the community's rehearsal for adulthood.

These are some of the most important themes that are found throughout many coming-of-age rituals; they are the threads that connect ceremonies—and societies—around the world.

CHAPTER
TWO   COMING-OF-AGE
        IN THE AMAZON

THE YANOMAMIS · The Yanomamis live deep within the Amazon rain forest in southern Venezuela and northern Brazil. They live primarily by planting, hunting animals, and gathering wild plants. Outsiders in search of gold, timber, and other natural resources have destroyed much of their land, threatened their way of life, and brought death to many Yanomamis. Since the late 1980s, many international environmental and Indian-rights groups have protested this destruction. Concerned groups from around the world are trying to help the Yanomamis, who proudly call themselves "the fierce people." To them, being fierce means being courageous.[1]

The Yanomamis live in villages of approximately seventy-five people who share a circular dwelling called a *shabano*. Each family lives in its own partitioned section within this structure. Members of the family hang their hammocks around the family hearth.

As a Yanomami girl grows up in the shabano, she may become engaged to several different men. Her family arranges the engagements, which are to accomplished hunters who are older than the girl. As a man's betrothed, the girl is expected to keep his fire burning and to bring him food.

Sexual relations are not part of this agreement, and a Yanomami girl may not marry until she begins to menstruate. She is said to come of age at the time of her first menses, and this event calls for her to participate in the most important ceremony of her life.

As do many similar cultures, the Yanomamis isolate a girl at the first sign of her menses. The Yanomamis believe that a female is powerful enough at this time to cause harm to any men she is around. For the rest of her life, a Yanomami female continues to stay in isolation from men each month during her menses.

At the onset of menstruation, a Yanomami girl is sent to a section of her house behind a barrier made of leaves and branches so that no men can see her. She also puts on new cotton garments that her mother and other older women in the shabano have made for her. Confinement to her quarters lasts at least a week, during which time she is expected to observe many traditional taboos, such as avoiding certain foods and some ways of preparing them.

In some groups, a Yanomami girl is required to eat with a stick that she cannot touch. To honor this custom, her female relatives feed her. They also prepare her fire and keep it burning for her. Grave consequences are expected if the fire ever goes out or the taboos are disobeyed.

Helena Valero is a Spanish woman who was kidnapped by the Yanomamis when she was a little girl and then lived among them for many years. Her story has helped outsiders to learn about their rituals.[2] According to Valero, when a Yanomami girl in her community comes of age she spends three weeks in isolation, during which time she is not allowed to talk or to cry.

When a girl's isolation period is over, the initiation structure is dismantled, and the girl is permitted to speak very softly. However, she is not supposed to look at males, lest her own developing female power endanger the men's physical abilities.

After a few more days, the girl's mother burns dried banana leaves near her and guides her in a walk around the fire. Then the initiate is permitted to speak normally once again. At that point, her mother and other women take the girl into the forest and decorate her in a traditional way. They wrap pieces of cotton around her arms and twist cotton around her waist and ankles. They also place a piece of white cotton around her chest.

When Yanomami girls are younger they have holes made in their earlobes, at the corners of their mouths, and in the middle of the lower lip. For the initiation, the women push strips of large yellow leaves through the holes in the girl's ears. They also put colored feathers through the holes near her mouth and in her lower lip. Her body is painted and if her hair is long, it is cut at this time. Her temporarily changed appearance lets everyone know that she is a new person, an initiate.

After she is painted, decorated, and dressed according to tradition, the girl is ready to enter the shabano. Followed by the other women, as well as by little girls, she slowly crosses the village plaza and goes to her mother's hearth. By taking this time-honored walk she lets the whole community know that she has become a young woman and is ready to marry.

After her coming-of-age ceremony, a Yano-mami female reveals her choice of a mate by hanging her hammock next to his. She might choose to marry one of the men she had been engaged to. Then again, she might decide on someone else altogether.

According to Napoleon Chagnon, an American anthropologist who has studied the Yanomamis for over twenty-five years, the transition into adulthood for males is not marked by a ceremony. However, Chagnon reports that when a Yanomami male feels he is ready to be treated like a man, he lets others know his wishes by the way he acts. He becomes annoyed when others call him by his personal name. This is because adult status among Yanomami males is established by how others speak to them, rather than by ritual.[3] Only children are called by their personal names.

The Yanomamis' special emphasis on female coming-of-age ceremonies may be due to the fact that their society has a shortage of women. A female's fertility is very important to them because she is the bearer of new life so that the Yanomamis can survive. A man seldom refuses to marry the woman who selects him to be her mate. From the onset of her first

A YANOMAMI GIRL IS PREPARED
FOR HER INITIATION.

menses to her marriage, the Yanomami female follows a path that emphasizes her fertility and value—a path that would promise survival were it not for the outsiders who threaten Yanomami tradition and life today.

TUKUNA FESTIVAL OF THE MÔÇA NOVA • Farther north in the Amazon live the Tukunas. They are fishermen with a strong belief in a spiritual world. They divide their world into a number of planes and realms—several underground worlds as well as many heavens. One of their most interesting myths is that of Ariana, a little girl who travels to all the cosmic realms and returns with the gift of maize for all of Earth's inhabitants.

This myth is paralleled in each Tukuna female's coming-of-age ritual, called the *Môça Nova* ("New Maiden"). During this festival, considered the most elaborate coming-of-age ceremony in South America, the initiate also travels through the cosmic realms and returns with gifts that are of great value to her people. The Môça Nova is the most important Tukuna ritual and certainly the most significant in a Tukuna girl's life. Yet, like the Yanomamis, the Tukunas have no significant initiation for males.

Another similarity to the Yanomamis is the Tukunas' isolation of the young woman when she has her first menses. But the isolation here is as much for the men's protection as it is for the girl's, since she is considered very vulnerable now to evil spirits who may whisk her away while she is undergoing her period of transformation.

When a Tukuna girl realizes that her menses has begun, she takes off her necklace and hangs it in her family's home where it can be easily seen. Then she hides in the forest near her home. Upon finding the necklace, the mother knows that her daughter has come of age, and she begins to search for her. The daughter is easily found because she taps two small sticks together to produce a special clacking sound. When the mother lovingly brings the girl back home, she places her on a special platform inside a shelter without walls that serves as a community center and is known as the big house.

The girl, now known as an initiate, or *voreki*, is to spend three months in her isolation chamber, from which she will emerge as a new person, an adult. But during her isolation she can only come out of hiding if no men are in the big house. To alert her to their presence so that she has time to hide, the men make sure to whistle when they come near.

The Tukunas believe that during her isolation, the initiate's soul wanders in the spirit world and is very susceptible to supernatural forces. Some may be good spirits, but evil spirits seek her out now, too. These include the *Noo*—the most ancient of all beings in Tukuna legends. The Noo live in an underworld connected to the earth by caves. The girl is said to risk great pain, even death, from the Noo if she disobeys the rituals or the taboos.

At the end of her seclusion, the girl is welcomed back into her community with a three-day festival complete with around-the-clock feasting, dancing, and drinking. Many guests come by canoe from far away to attend the festival, which is hosted by one of the girl's uncles on her father's side. The uncle greets the guests, each of whom brings a hammock to hang near the dance floor in the big house. Guests also bring their own food, since the host is only required to provide the drinks.

Even though many guests are present now, the voreki is still considered in danger from the Noo. She stays secluded in a small round hut made of palm leaves that has been specially constructed inside the big house for the occasion.

This cocoonlike structure represents the underworld, through which the girl is said to travel, bravely facing its dangers. But the underworld is not the only journey taken by the initiate. The hut's outside walls are painted with special designs, among them the sun, moon, morning star, and a deer. The first three symbols represent the girl's exit from the underworld into the heavenly realm. The deer symbolizes watchfulness, and reminds the Tukunas to carefully guard the young woman. The deer also has a role in Tukuna legends as a wild creature that is transformed into a peaceful, productive animal. This dramatic change, from immature to mature being, is symbolic of what the initiate undergoes.

Musicians play drums and trumpets (*uaricánas*) as well as wind instruments, which produce a ghostly sound believed to be the voice of the Noo. The uaricánas are massive 20-foot (6-meter) instruments made from hollow palm logs. They are among the Tukunas' most sacred possessions. Only men can play them or even look at them. (For that reason the uaricánas are only played at night. During the day the men hide them in the forest where the women cannot find them.)

The musical instruments serve a spiritual as well as a protective purpose. According to legend, if the rhythmic beat is missed, the girl's danger from the Noo will grow.

The spirits are present in the dramatic cloth masks made from tree bark that many of the male guests wear, as well as in the music. The masks represent evil people-eating spirits described in Tukuna legends. Some masqueraders wear 8-foot-tall (2.5-meter) costumes that symbolize the demons of the jungle. Others are disguised as demon monkeys and jaguars. The true identity of each masquerader is concealed until the festival is almost over. These masked guests race about, breaking things with their clubs and shaking the outside of the isolation hut. Yet there is a playfulness about their antics; the monsters are a bit like pranksters.

For the first two days of the ceremony, the initiate's family keeps a close watch over her, so that the dangerous demons cannot get near. Guarding the voreki is as necessary as keeping up a constant musical beat. Musicians cannot take a break unless they find someone else to take their place.

Meanwhile, inside her hut, the young woman has her whole body painted with a special black dye as protection against the Noo. She is also painted with red *urucu*, the favorite body paint of many native peoples of the Amazon. Her ceremonial costume includes hawk feathers that are glued to her skin, and a short cotton skirt with a wide belt, from which many strings of glass beads hang. Bracelets, fringes, and tassels adorn her. The tassels are woven of the spectacular feathers of toucans, macaws, and other brilliantly colored birds.

But no part of her outfit is more magnificent than her headdress. This striking creation is made mainly from the bright red tail feathers of the macaw. The feathers serve as an emblem of the sun, which is very important to the Tukunas. It represents

DURING A TUKUNA GIRL'S COMING-OF-AGE RITUAL,
MASKED DANCERS REPRESENTING LEGENDARY SPIRITS
PLAYFULLY ATTACK THE INITIATE'S HUT.

creative energy. Reaching its realm is the girl's goal. However, she is forbidden to look at the sun until she has earned the right to bask in its full glory. For that reason, the headdress is lowered over her eyes when it is first put on.4

The girl is secluded until the third day. Early that morning, before dawn, her uncle cuts an opening in the hut. Then he and the girl's mother lead her out, holding her tightly. Other relatives join in, to help protect her from the Noo, who are considered most dangerous to her now.

When the girl is safely outside, her relatives dance with her until dawn to keep the masked demons away. Then, as day breaks, the voreki is released by her protectors. Now her feather crown is lifted above her eyes so that she can see the rising sun. Then a shaman (medicine man) hands the girl a piece of burning wood—a firebrand—that he tells her to throw against a tree trunk. The firebrand serves as a weapon for her; its fire symbolizes that of the sun. By obeying the order, the young woman destroys the evil spirits' power over her. At last she is safe! Her relatives no longer need to protect her. She has survived the isolation and overcome the evil spirits.

But the ceremony is not over yet. Now everyone goes inside, where the girl sits on a mat in the center of the floor. Then, at about noon, her uncle pulls a lock of hair from her head. This is just the start. As drums beat, Tukuna women follow suit, plucking out all of the girl's hair except for a single red-dyed lock. This is pulled out by the girl's uncle.5 A recent investigation suggests that this painful ordeal may have been inspired by the Tukuna legend of Ariana, who is said to have pulled out two locks of hair from the sun. Other interpretations are that the act is a symbolic death, a sacrifice, or a public display of strength.[6]

After the ordeal is over, the masqueraders remove their costumes and give them to the girl. Now they become human again, as shown by their ability to eat the gift of smoked meat they now receive. Evil spirits eat their meat raw; cooked meat is said to be a sign of civilization.

Before the ceremony ends, anyone present with magic power, such as that of healing the sick, will focus it on the girl to give her added protection. Then she is taken down to the river, where she is bathed by the shamans. Following this, the guests destroy the isolation hut and throw it into the river. Then they merrily push each other into the water, usually with much hilarity and relief now that the dramatic events of the past few days are over. Afterward, guests will help to clean up and then head for home.

More ritualistic ceremonies may take place after the guests have left. These final events involve other myths from the past. One includes taking a bath with a solution of *timbo*, a plant that is considered a poison because it causes fish to die. Timbo represents moderation; besides being a poison it is also believed to cause women to be temporarily infertile and thus serves as a contraceptive. According to one re-

THE INITIATE'S FACE IS DAUBED WITH URUCU
DYE AFTER SHE HAS SUFFERED THE ORDEAL OF
HAVING HER HAIR PLUCKED OUT.

searcher, the reason for this bath may lie in the fact that for fishing people, unrestrained fertility could result in too many people, which in turn would wipe out the fish. By taking the bath the initiate may be renouncing temporarily the conception of children, and thus allowing the fish population to continue to thrive.[7]

Following the ceremony, the young woman is permitted to marry, although she usually waits until her hair has grown back. In sharp contrast to the elaborate ceremony she has just been through, there is no wedding feast. In fact, probably nothing in the young woman's life will equal her unforgettable Môça Nova. What could possibly match an event during which she travels through many realms, bravely overcomes evil spirits, brings her people the gift of her own fertility, and at the same time gains a broader perspective, so that she uses such gifts wisely and in moderation? It is through the festival of the Môça Nova that she earns the privilege of taking her place in the balance of nature as a Tukuna woman.

CHAPTER
THREE   COMING-OF-AGE
IN TRIBAL AFRICA

THE SAN · The San are a tribal people who once inhabited all of southern Africa. They are also known as Bushmen, a term the San consider derogatory since it was given to them by Dutch settlers some three hundred years ago. When other people— whites from Europe and blacks from elsewhere in Africa—settled in South Africa, they pushed the San north from their native lands. Today, almost all of the 70,000 or so remaining San live in a vast, desolate stretch of African desert known as the Kalahari. This barren land runs primarily through Botswana and Namibia. The San's traditional hunter-gatherer lifestyle is rapidly disappearing. Outsiders have affected every aspect of their tribal life, including coming-of-age rituals.

In San society, women and men are treated as equals, although this, too, is changing. In the past, women played a crucial role in the survival of the bands, because the women's gathering provided most

SAN GIRLS FROM THE KALAHARI DESERT. TO THE SAN,
WHO ONCE SURVIVED SOLELY ON HUNTING AND GATHERING,
A MENSTRUATING WOMAN WAS A SERIOUS THREAT TO A
MAN'S PROWESS AS A HUNTER.

of the San's food. Knowledge of edible plants was extremely valuable, since the food supply varied dramatically from one season to the next.

Today, herders and farmers have driven many of the larger game animals away. Only about one thousand San are able to maintain a semblance of their traditional lifestyle as hunters and gatherers. San men often work as cattle herders and as unskilled laborers. The women, who now have fewer plants to gather, either depend on their husbands or work on settlers' farms. The few rituals that are still held are remnants of the past, when small bands of San would move from water hole to water hole and fully exercise their desert skills.

The San are divided into several groups. These include the !Kung, Kua, Gw/i and !XU (the marks ! and / refer to clicks and pops in their spoken language). The !Kung are a San people who live in northern Botswana and in neighboring areas of Namibia and Angola. Once again, it is the !Kung women who have the more involved coming-of-age ritual.

Each female is isolated during her first menstruation, as in the Yanomami and Tukuna tribes. A !Kung woman stays in a hut with an older woman who looks after her. The young woman is forbidden to look at men or the sun. She avoids men lest her new power endanger them, and she avoids the sun because to the !Kung, a desert people, its scorching rays represent death. (In contrast, to the Tukunas and other tribal groups who live in more temporate climates, the sun symbolizes life.)

Most of the !Kung ceremonies are held only after the sun goes down. While the young woman is secluded in her special hut, women and old men do the Eland Dance with its special First Menstruation steps and songs. The Eland Dance is named for the twigs the male dancers fasten to their heads to represent the horns of the eland, the biggest of Africa's antelopes. The !Kung believe that the eland has more supernatural power than any other creature.

When her first period is over, the girl is washed and rubbed with fats and oils, and her face is painted with red powder. Now she may leave her shelter and return to her normal life. However, the ritual is not yet over. The first time she drinks water or eats food from a plant, the final part of the First Menstruation takes place.

An older woman, often her mother, scrapes a root into the water hole. Then, taking the young woman's hand, she chews the root. Together they cook plant foods in the fire and eat them. Here is another common theme in rites of passage—the sharing of food.

After her coming-of-age ceremony is over, the young woman wears red paint around her eyes as a sign that she is free to marry. During future menstruations, the initiate is no longer required to go into seclusion, but she must obey certain taboos. She cannot touch any weapons used for hunting, for to do so is said to lessen the power of the hunter. She is also required to abstain from making love with her husband, since at this time she might rob him of the desire to go hunting.

For most San, the loss of traditional lands and food sources has stripped these rituals of their meaning. But today, the coming-of-age ceremony for !Kung boys, known as *Choma*, is still observed in simplified form. Held in the winter at four- or five-year intervals, this group ceremony is not mandatory; a boy can refuse to take part in it if he chooses. However, only boys who have shot their first buck are eligible to join.

Choma is held near the village. Only men and boys can participate. For several days, they perform special dances. At the end of that time, each boy has a vertical line painted in the middle of his forehead, and he receives a special haircut. These are signs to all who see him that he has experienced Choma and is close to manhood.

In the past, when animals were plentiful, each maturing boy used to prepare for a much more important ceremony. This took place when he killed a large animal. Until he performed this feat, called the Rite of the First Kill, and brought the animal's meat to his future in-laws, a boy could not become a husband. His future wife's parents wanted to know that he would be able to hunt and thus provide for their daughter, as well as for them in their old age. And the boy wanted to successfully perform the Rite of the First Kill because he would not be considered a man unless he married.

Boys prepared for the Rite of the First Kill by listening carefully when the men sat around the camp fire and talked about the animals they had killed. Boys also practiced tracking small animals and killing them with a bow and arrow.

Traditionally, each !Kung boy went through the Rite of the First Kill twice in his lifetime—once when he brought down his first big male animal and again when he killed his first big female prey.

At the rite, traditional cuts were made in the young man's chest, back, and arms. Herbal medicine mixed with the fat of the animal he had killed was rubbed into the cuts. The medicine in his chest cuts was said to make him want to be a hunter, in his arms it gave him good aim, in his back it kept the animal from escaping, and on his brow it helped him spot the animal quickly.

The cuts produced permanent scars—a symbol of the value the !Kung once placed on hunting as well as a permanent sign of the young man's passage into manhood. The parents of the young woman to whom he was betrothed then accepted him as their son-in-law. The whole community learned the good news when the young man's future father-in-law distributed the meat he received from the young man to the group.

Today this traditional rite of passage, when it is held at all, has only symbolic meaning. The !Kung are struggling for their spiritual existence. Although with help from others they are able to survive, their culture is suffering because the customs that once unified the people and generations have all but disappeared.

THE MBUTI · Some thirteen different groups of short people—approximately 4 feet 8 inches (1.4 meters) tall—are scattered throughout central Africa. Although they are often called Pygmies, they consider this name to be derogatory and prefer being known by the name of their specific group. One of these is the Mbuti, 50,000 of whom live in the Ituri Forest of what is now Zaire.

The Mbuti were the first known inhabitants of this region. Today these muscular people exist in small bands, and their livelihood is a combination of hunting and gathering mixed with trading and some cash exchanges.

For many generations, the various Mbuti have had a cooperative trade relationship with the Bantu and Sudanic villagers who live near them. The Mbuti bring the villagers food from the forest; meat and honey are especially prized. In return, the villagers cultivate many foods for the Mbuti in their gardens. The villagers are also the Mbuti's source for such items as cotton, clothing, soap, and salt.

Equally important, the villagers protect the Mbuti and help them organize some of their major rituals and ceremonies. The villagers and Mbuti have some of the same rituals; they hold other rituals together, which serves as a way of binding one generation after another to the tradition of economic co-operation.

Within each Mbuti band, survival depends upon everyone—children and adults, women and men—working together in harmony. Women are responsible for gathering plants as well as tending the huts, doing the cooking, and caring for children. The men are the hunters.

Both the Mbuti and the villagers have a ritual for girls when they come of age. The Mbuti consider menstruation a special gift, and the *elima* is one of their most joyful occasions. In contrast to many other hunter-gatherer societies that fear a woman's power when she comes of age, the Mbuti happily acknowledge that a girl who is "blessed with the blood" is now a potential wife and mother. The elima is held at the onset of a girl's menses, and it lasts for anywhere from a week to a month or more.

According to Colin Turnbull, a renowned chronicler of the Mbuti, a young woman is confined to a hut at this time, but she is not isolated, as Yanomami and Tukuna females are.[1] Her girlfriends join her, whether they have reached maturity or not. The friends are under the watchful eyes of older women, who protect and care for them as well as teach them special elima songs. In the hut, the girls learn the women's songs, as well as lessons about the future responsibilities of those who have reached childbearing age. All the while, they must obey certain taboos, such as those about the kinds of food they may eat.

Although the elima celebrates a girl's puberty, it is the closest the Mbuti men have to a coming-of-age ritual of their own. While the girls are busy inside the hut, eligible young Mbuti bachelors gather outside. Some of the elima songs call for the young men to respond in song. They do this while waiting for a look at the young women inside.

At night, the girls and young women sing their songs and dance outside the hut while their mothers and older sisters guard them. Nevertheless, the elima participants manage to sneak glances at the young men around them. In daylight, the elima participants periodically emerge from the hut with stout whips in their hands. If a young woman who has reached puberty chases down an eligible bachelor and strikes him with a whip, he is supposed to visit her in the elima hut. This is easier said than done, since it is traditional for the young man to have to fight his way in (even if the young woman very much wants him to visit).

Once inside, if a young man loves the young woman who struck him, and if he has received her mother's consent, he may lie down beside her. This is a sign that the couple is engaged, and the young man is not permitted to leave the elima house until the festival is over. However, marriage will not be allowed until the young man brings his future in-laws meat from a large animal. As with the traditional !Kung, a young Mbuti male must prove to his potential in-laws that he has the ability to support a wife, as well as provide for them when they grow old.

While many elima ceremonies take place only among Mbuti girls, others are held for both village and forest girls together. For instance, an eastern group of Mbuti called the Efe have a special ceremony for young women whose fathers have been partners in trade with villagers known as the Lese. This shared experience binds the young women to each other for life.

The ceremony generally takes place only if the village girl's father is very wealthy, since a village elima is much more expensive than one held in the forest. The young women must be provided for during the months they are in the elima hut, and the huge dance and feast celebrating the young women's release from isolation is costly.

Their mothers weave beautifully colored and patterned bark belts, breast bands, and arm straps for the girls to wear. Cloth made from pounded bark was once the Mbuti's everyday dress. Now it has been replaced by Western clothes and is worn only for special ceremonies such as the elima.[2] As in the elimas held only for Mbuti, the grand finale of an elima sponsored by a villager is a ceremonial feast at which the young women sing with the older women to signify their adult status. Now mothers and grandmothers welcome the young women back as grownups.

Although the elima serves as the Mbuti's initiation for young men as well as for young girls, the villagers expect male Mbuti to go through another coming-of-age ceremony, known as *nkumba*. This is the villagers' group initiation into adult society. In general, agricultural societies such as those of the villagers tend to have group initiations rather than individual ones. The nkumba lasts about two months and takes place every three years in the villages.

All boys—villagers and Mbuti—between the ages of eight and twelve must participate in the ritual. Observers report that the ceremony is perceived very differently by the Mbuti and by the villagers. For the villagers, the nkumba is the traditional way to acknowledge adulthood, as well as to unite with and win favor from their ancestors. Only initiated villagers can join their ancestors when they die. This is very important to the villagers, because the dead are considered an integral part of their community; they are thought to dwell among the living, only in a different dimension.

On the other hand, the Mbuti consider the nkumba as merely a formality—an obligation to be fulfilled so that the villagers will respect their maturity and continue to cooperate with the tribe in economic matters.

The Efe, an eastern band of the nomadic Mbuti,
have made camp at the edge of the Ituri forest in Zaire.
Ancient Egyptian records show that the Mbuti have
been in this area for some 4,500 years.

The ceremony involves circumcision. In the Ituri Forest, as in many other places where circumcision is observed, the boys are expected to be brave and try to not cry when the surgery is performed. Each operation on a Mbuti boy is followed by one on a village boy, binding the two in a blood brotherhood for life. This closeness between the two young men is useful when the two become trading partners as their fathers were before them.

The circumcision and the tests of physical endurance that follow are believed necessary to toughen initiates for adult life. All these events take place at an initiation camp. Here, each boy is taught work songs and special dances. Village men dance while tapping out a rhythm with ceremonial sticks called *makatis*.

Ritual acts include shaving the head to symbolize the casting off of an old life. As in the elima hut, the initiates observe traditional taboos. These include rules about what the boys eat, as well as how and with whom they dine. They are not supposed to eat with their hands or to sit down to eat with their initiated relatives.

However, after Colin Turnbull had witnessed the Mbuti's initiation, he reported that they obeyed the taboos only while their hosts were present. When the villagers had left, the Mbuti boys ate foods forbidden to them, dined with their choice of companions, used their fingers while eating, and did other things they had been told were taboo. But Turnbull felt that the boys did not mean to show disrespect by disobeying. Rather, the taboos and the ritual had no meaning to them. Although the villagers expect the Mbuti to accept the unseen power of the village tribal ancestors, the Mbuti have their own traditions to follow.

After the initiation, the villagers treat the Mbuti as men. Yet, when the Mbuti go back to their forest home, they are still treated as boys by their tribe. They are still forbidden to join in the special songs that the men sing. Not until a boy kills a large antelope and presents it to his in-laws is his manhood accepted by his people. This is similar to the !Kung tradition and suits the needs of a society of nomadic hunter-gatherers.

THE MASAI · The Masai are mostly a pastoral and seminomadic people who live today on both sides of the Kenya-Tanzania border. Their name derives from their language, known as Maa. For centuries, the Masai roamed freely from the deserts north of Mount Kenya to the plains south of Mount Kilimanjaro and from the beaches of the Indian Ocean to the shores of Lake Victoria. Although the arrival of Europeans in Africa limited their wanderings, these tall, proud warriors, lion hunters, and cattle herders have resisted change. Many of them continue to live as their ancestors did.

The Masai raise sheep and goats for meat. But their livelihood revolves around dairy cattle, which they usually raise and sometimes raid from other tribal groups. Many stories are told about the raids of Masai warriors, whom others both fear and admire.

There are now approximately 100,000 Masai. Their male-dominated society is structured around four roles: junior warrior, senior warrior, junior elder, and senior elder. The warriors defend the people in times of war and serve the community in peacetime. Each generation of boys forms an age-set, and all the boys in an age-set are circumcised at the same time.[3]

As part of their coming-of-age ritual, Masai girls undergo a clitoridectomy. From ten years of age until their first menstruation and the operation that follows, Masai girls live in *manyattas*. These are also the camps for the boys who are warriors. The girls' lives at the camps are carefree until their menses and clitoridectomy bring an end to their happy-go-lucky days. Soon after circumcision, the girls are married. Masai girls cannot be married unless they undergo this operation. However, a Masai girl's parents may already have arranged her engagement to a warrior before the ritual. In this case, she receives gifts before the operation.

It is preferred that warriors and uncircumcised girls do not engage in sexual relations. However, if a couple does have relations and the girl becomes pregnant, she will not be able to marry until she has a clitoridectomy.

The female circumcision takes place inside the hut with older women in attendance. Although the government of Kenya has banned this operation, Masai women are still circumcised, and the operation is very much a part of their culture. While the young woman heals from the operation she wears a special headband that identifies her as *enkaibartani*, "one who awaits healing." After she has healed, her head is shaved in a ritual so that all the families in her *enkang*, or settlement, can see she is becoming a woman, and a two-day celebration filled with dancing and singing takes place.

Masai warriors, known as *moran*, are circumcised in a ritual that marks their initiation into manhood and the freedoms and respect that go along with it. There is great pride in being moran. Women admire the warriors, and elders look back at their own warrior days with nostalgia.[4] Many boys urge their fathers to have them circumcised.

The fathers have mixed feelings. Once their sons are moran, they can no longer tell them what to do. Then, too, the ceremony cannot take place until the fathers perform a ceremony called "passing over the fence." This symbolizes a father's willingness to accept the status of an "old man." So, among the Masai, a young man's passage into adulthood affects not only himself, but also the status of his father.

Like the nkumba celebrated by the Mbuti and their villager trading partners, the Masai boys' circumcision is a group ritual. A respected elder man who has knowledge of the supernatural as well as the Masai world educates the boys for three months in a camp that is separated from their village. He teaches them the customs of their people and the duties of the warrior. Then they return to their village for the circumcision ritual, which is a public ceremony, although no females may attend.

The initiates' appearance is a visible sign to everyone that a change in status is in process. Each initiate has had his head shaved and wears ceremonial clothes, which may include a leather cape and many necklaces. The moran, greased with red ocher for the occasion, sing special songs and perform special dances. However, they do not play instruments. (The Masai's only instrument is a long, curved kudu horn that is only used at the moran graduation ceremony.)

A Masai initiation ceremony, one of the many group rituals that prepare a Masai boy for his new status as a warrior, or moran.

After their initiation, the boys paint their faces with white clay so that they won't be mistaken for girls, whose heads are also shaved. Later, when the boys' hair grows back, they will be called moran. As moran they team up with the other boys who have been circumcised with them to form a closely knit age-set whose members remain loyal to each other for life.

In the old days, moran could expect to defend the tribe and to help raid cattle when Masai herds were low in number. Today, things have changed. Because there are generally no enemies to fend off, warriors mostly roam about in small bands, fighting sporadic skirmishes, stealing cattle, and hunting lions. Lion hunting is especially important; a boy who kills a lion is a hero to his people.

There will be a second initiation, after which the boys will go to live in the manyattas. These camps are built by the warriors' mothers. Here the boys receive instructions from their elders, while their mothers act as chaperones for the uncircumcised girls who live there, too. During the day, the moran practice their skills at wrestling, throwing clubs, and using spears, swords, and shields. At night they dance and sing with the girls. Hairdressing is another popular activity, since the young men's elaborate hairstyles require many hours of work. Bits of wool are twisted into their hair to fashion their distinctive style.

The moran have many rules to follow, most of them intended to teach the boys discipline and to unify the group. For instance, moran are not permitted to eat or drink alone. They are also forbidden to have sexual relations with the girls. However, as mentioned earlier, this is not always obeyed.

Groups of boys and men are divided by age, with each age group consisting of all the boys circumcised within a certain period of time. The most prestigious group in the manyattas are the seniors. Not until a male is a senior does he have the right to marry. As younger boys become moran, the seniors graduate, and junior moran replace them in rank. In the manyatta, young men are seniors for seven years, during which time the younger moran compete with them in contests of skill. When seniors graduate, the event is acknowledged in the *Eunoto*, the elaborate warrior graduation ceremony. During this occasion their hair is shaved off by their mothers.

After a boy leaves the manyatta he will be a junior elder and, later on in life, a senior elder. Throughout all these stages, he will belong to a particular age-set composed of his closest peers.

Today, formal education is starting to change Masai life. More and more Masai children are foregoing the traditional rites of passage and going to school instead. Relations between moran and Masai schoolchildren are often strained. The moran say that the other boys are cowards, while the students call the moran who refuse formal education "illiterates."5 In fact, all of the Masai children are students, whether they learn out in the camps or in the schoolhouse.

However, as the need for defense diminishes for the Masai, their traditional coming-of-age rituals are bound to change.

CHAPTER FOUR AUSTRALIAN ABORIGINES

Aborigines are the descendants of the first Australians, who are believed to have come to that continent in rafts or boats from southeastern Asia at least 40,000 years ago. The Aborigines once had Australia all to themselves. From generation to generation they passed on a unique culture that attributes all creations to the ancients—legendary ancestors who lived in a long-ago past called Dreamtime.

When the Europeans first came to Australia, approximately 300,000 Aborigines were living there. Many of them died, in large part due to epidemics of deadly diseases unknowingly brought by the foreigners. The Aborigines were also run off their land by farmers and sheep and cattle herders. Today there are some 160,000 Aborigines left, about 50,000 of them full-blooded. Many contemporary Aborigines are involved in an ongoing struggle to secure respect, recognition, and equal rights with other Australians.

Aborigines are renowned for their elaborate coming-of-age rituals for boys. Some of their ancient traditions have been lost, and others have changed over time to fit the demands of modern society. Knowledge about those that do remain is a closely guarded secret, concealed from outsiders as well as from the uninitiated among their own people. Although many Aborigines are being integrated into mainstream Australian society, in the "outback," away from the cities, Aborigine men continue to participate in initiation rites. Women also have secret rituals, but even less is known about their ceremonies than those of the men.

Although coming-of-age rituals differ from group to group, the Aruntas of central Australia perform a ceremony that is typical of many other Aborigine tribes. It is during this ritual that boys are allowed to start learning the secrets of their people. The Aborigine process of initiation heralds the beginning of a learning experience that will continue throughout a male's life.

Outsiders do not know how often the Aruntas hold their coming-of-age rituals today. They used to be performed for all boys between the ages of ten and twelve. The Arunta rituals, which include several different ceremonies and span many years, mark a boy's transition from boyhood to manhood while also bringing him the power and approval of the ancients. By participating in the ritual, Aborigines are assured that life will continue on for them as it has since the rituals were first performed in the Dreamtime. The mood associated with these rites is one of deep reverence.

Arunta initiations are held at a special camp for

men. Each boy is taken there after being dramatically snatched from the women of his family, who wail as they watch him set out to meet his fate. But this wailing is partly an act; each mother knows that her role is to deeply etch the occasion in her son's mind. This creates a very emphatic separation between the boy's dependence on his mother and his life as an adult. [1]

During an Arunta boy's first ceremony, men and women await his arrival at a sacred place near the main camp. The men toss the boy into the air several times, while the women sing and shout as they dance around the group. His relatives paint special patterns on his body. These, he is told, will quicken his growing up. The men also tell him that he can no longer play with girls and women. Now he has to leave his family and live in the men's camp.

Although the paints are only temporary, the boy is also marked by several permanent body signs of his new status in the tribe. These include a cut in the boy's nasal septum so that he can start wearing a nose-bone.

The first ceremony may take place when the boy is still a child, whereas the next ceremony will be held after he has reached puberty and lasts for several days. The Aborigines hold many dances, known as *corrobborees*, during which older males represent the ancients and chant stories about heroes from that special time.

When the ceremonial ground has been readied in a place hidden from the women, some of the boy's tribal kin grab him and take him there. Now the boy begins learning the secrets of his tribe, secrets that he is warned not to divulge to anyone. If he does, something terrible will surely happen to him and his relatives.

During the early part of this ceremony, the boy receives a lighted wooden stick from his future mother-in-law. (His future bride was selected for him when he was much younger.) As he holds the burning stick he is told that he must always hold fast to his own fire. In other words, he must always be faithful to his wife. Then the boy returns to the male camp, accompanied by his ceremonial guides, as well as the women and younger boys.

Four days later, the boy begins to witness many secret rituals performed over a three-day period on ceremonial ground. These are reenactments from Aborigine history, filled with the mystery and wonder of a rich mythological past. Since the Aborigines have no written language, these ceremonies serve as a way of passing knowledge from generation to generation. The meaning of each performance is revealed to the boy.

Then, during the days to come, he is taken hunting by his guides, who chant songs about the ancients' deeds and who take him to still more performances, during which he is forbidden to speak unless he is spoken to. His mission now is to concentrate on the performances and their revelations about the ancestral symbols that unite his people.

AN ABORIGINE PLAYS A HORN AT A
RITUAL DANCE DURING WHICH LISTENERS
ARE REMINDED OF THEIR LEGENDARY
PAST CALLED THE DREAMTIME.

When the rituals are over, the adult women join the celebrants. But instead of receiving a warm welcome, the men pelt them with pieces of bark. Here, another important drama is played out that further symbolizes the boy's removal from the influence of women. After participating in still more ceremonies, the women return to the camp for the last time.

Now the ceremonial ground fills with the sound of bull-roarers. A bull-roarer is a piece of wood with a hole in it that is tied to a string and whirled. The women, children, and initiates believe that the sound produced by swinging the bull-roarers is the voice of the spirit that will help the boy recover after he is circumcised. Thus, everyone who hears the sound knows that the time of circumcision is near.

After the operation is performed, the men congratulate the boy on his bravery, and the bull-roarers are placed against the wound. The initiate now learns that the true source of the sound is the bull-roarers and not the spirits, as the women and children still believe. He also learns about *churingas*, round pieces of stone or wood that are the Arunta's most sacred objects. Because the ancients are believed to dwell in them, these objects represent the closest bond possible between the Arunta and their Dreamtime ancestors. The boy is warned that the churingas must never be shown to or discussed with women and children.

Other young men who have been recently initiated are now brought to the ceremonial ground to have their backs scraped with a churinga. This is meant to make them friends for life. Then the initiate's ceremonial guides take him back to the men's camp, where he stays until his wound heals.

After his recovery, a second genital operation is held. Known in surgical terms as subincision, this operation involves cutting a slit in the penis. Anthropologists, psychologists, and others have pondered the reason for this operation. Some suggest it is for hygienic reasons. Others say that it is performed to win further favor with the tribal gods by virtue of the extreme sacrifice and pain. Like the first genital operation, the second involves many rituals. No women are present for any of them. When the second operation is over, the initiate has earned a new status. He is called an *Ertwa-kurka*.

The next phase of the ritual begins when the boy has recovered from his second operation. He walks up to the main camp, surrounded by a group of men who have participated in the ceremonies. The men sing loudly. When the women hear them, they come out and dance near the men. Their approach prompts the men to start shouting "Tirra, tirra, tirra," a sound resembling that made by the bull-roarers. The women echo this sound.

Now the Ertwa-kurka emerges from the group of men, runs up to the women, then quickly turns and runs away into the bush. Several men follow him and spend the night with him, singing until shortly before daybreak.

Meanwhile, the Ertwa-kurka's guides help him put on ceremonial clothes, which include a shield and a spear thrower. Then he sets out, surrounded by men shouting "Tirra, tirra, tirra!" When they near the women, the men step back, so that the newly initiated young man walks alone. His face hidden behind his shield, he gets closer and closer to the women until his female relatives reach out and cut off some locks of his hair. These they later make into ornaments that they wear as mementoes of the day. Then he goes back to the men.

This ceremony earns the Ertwa-kurka the privilege of joining the elders who hold the ceremonies. However, he shows them respect by not speaking loudly in their presence, and several months will pass before he can speak directly to them.

The initiation is not over yet. The next day the young man is decorated, and then he carries a boomerang with him as he approaches the women. When he is close enough to them, he throws the boomerang in the direction from which his mother's ancestors are said to have come in the Dreamtime. This is another symbol of the boy becoming free of his mother's control.

A three-day rite of silence follows. Each day brings the young man nearer to his goal of becoming a fully initiated member of the tribe. His last rite is known as *Engwura*. This multiphased ceremony includes performances reenacting the tribe's history. During the time the young man goes through this last series of events, he is not supposed to eat very much nor to be too comfortable. His endurance will test his courage, and his sacrifices will please the gods.

One highlight of the Engwura ceremonies is the fire ordeal in which the young man has to lie down upon the smoking boughs of a fire from which he cannot arise unless the elders allow him to. Only after this ordeal are young men given not only full manhood but also full adult status as an *Urliara* in the tribe.

When the initiate returns to the camp as a man, a big corrobboree is held in his honor. Coming-of-age rituals will continue at set intervals for the rest of a male's life.

Although this gradual initiation may seem challenging and painful to outsiders, Aborigine elders believe that a young man who is slowly led through the legendary history of his tribe gains self-esteem, as well as respect for his place in the group and for the group itself. By observing the conduct and bearing of his elders during the ceremonies, the young man learns to respect them and to appreciate the significance of each performance he witnesses.

Today, as Aborigines appear to be forsaking these traditions, the elders mourn the loss of rituals that test the strength and character of their young men. In many ways, it is the deep and intricate connections forged by these male rituals that create the unique identity of these people.

CHAPTER FIVE

NATIVE AMERICAN COMING-OF-AGE RITUALS

When European explorers first came to North America, they found many native tribes living on the continent. Most of these groups survived through hunting and fishing or gathering plants. The Pueblo tribes of the Southwest were entirely agricultural, while the Apaches and Navajos were nomadic hunter-gatherer societies. Tribes of the Eastern Woodlands, who were scattered from the Great Lakes region in the North all the way down to the tip of present-day Florida, combined farming with hunting, fishing, and gathering plants. Basically, the lay of the land dictated the social structure.

   The lives of these Native Americans were enriched by their ceremonies, which were often a form of worship. Many tribes honored the Great Spirit that created everything—the Earth, human life, plants and animals, as well as the various spirit forms of wind, fire, air, and water. Most Native Americans shared a belief in the magical power of nature; to them everything was alive and connected.[1]

Like the Australian Aborigines, Native Americans were ravaged by diseases brought by Europeans, against which they had no natural immunities. Other destructive forces were alcohol, warfare, forced relocation, and the demise of traditional lifestyles. Tribes were often coerced into signing peace treaties that resulted in the loss of their lands in return for supposed benefits that were promised, but rarely received.

Today, Native Americans continue to face tremendous challenges. An estimated 31 percent of Native Americans live below the poverty level, with the unemployment rate on the reservations at 45 percent. Their rate of alcoholism is reportedly about twice that of non-Indians.[2] Although their problems are great, more and more Native Americans are making their voices heard as they struggle to assert their unique identity.

In recent years, ceremonies that were either abandoned or driven underground have resurfaced. Despite the assimilation of many Native Americans into mainstream society, the elders in many tribal groups or nations continue to hold centuries-old rituals and to pass them on to the next generation. By doing so, the various Native American groups remain linked to their past and to the land, as well as to its spirits.

Coming-of-age rituals vary among the many different Native American cultures. In the past, when girls began to menstruate, a number of tribes isolated them for a period of time. Later, throughout their childbearing years, females were kept away from males during their monthly menstruation because they were considered powerful enough at that time to endanger the hunters and warriors.

NORTHWEST COASTAL TRIBES · In some Native American tribes on the Pacific Northwest Coast, such as the Tlingit, Tsimshian, and Haida, girls were confined to a dark hideaway, sometimes for as long as a year or more, at the onset of menses. During that time they saw only certain female relatives. Because the girls were considered very powerful, they had to remain hooded when they left their retreat so that they wouldn't harm people, hunting and fishing equipment, or nature itself.

Native American girls of the Pacific Northwest Coast who were approaching puberty also had to fast for a customary number of days and obey food taboos, some of which lasted for years. These included a ban on eating fresh salmon, the main food along the coast.

Until early in the twentieth century, young women from wealthier families of the Northwest Coast groups received their first labret during puberty. A labret is a lip ornament made out of wood or stone. When it was inserted, everyone could tell at a glance that the wearer was of marriageable age.

Among several Northwest Coast groups, an elaborate feast and social event, known as a *potlatch*, continues to be held to commemorate a variety of events, including mourning for a deceased family member and celebration of a new social status in the tribe. It has also served some Kwakiutl and Tlingit groups as a puberty rite.

Potlatches are ceremonies at which enormous

quantities of food are consumed, many performances take place, and many presents are given to the guests. The types of gifts, as well as the lavishness of the ceremony, reflect the host's economic standing, wealth being of great importance to the Northwest Coast tribes. Although Canadian and United States government laws have attempted to prohibit potlatches, they continue to this day.

THE SIOUX · In many tribes, great respect for women is shown in the special coming-of-age ceremonies held for them. The Sioux, on the Great Plains, consider a girl's puberty a major event because women are the cornerstone of the Sioux family. Many Sioux groups believe that their female puberty ceremony is one of the Seven Sacred Rites given to the Sioux by their guiding force, known as *Wakantanka,* or the Great Spirit.

In the past, when a Sioux girl came of age, she was first isolated in a small shelter, where an older female (usually her mother) instructed her in the necessary women's tasks of her time. If her family was rich, her isolation would end with a sumptuous feast in her honor.

At this feast, the shaman chanted to White Buffalo Calf Woman, one of the powerful guardian spirits who served as a messenger between human beings and the Great Spirit. Then he informed the girl of her adult responsibilities and placed a sacred eagle feather in her hair. The feather was a symbol of her new status. Now everyone considered her to be a woman. The ceremony in a modified form is still held by some traditional families as a symbol of a girl's coming of age.

THE APACHES · Today, the Apaches and their cousins the Navajos of the Southwest hold two of the best-known Native American puberty ceremonies for girls.

The Western Apaches call their ceremony the Sunrise Dance and generally conduct it for several girls at the same time. During the four-day event, many ritual chants and dances, as well as feasting, entertainment, and gift-giving, take place. The girls who are being honored are not allowed to bathe, touch their skin, or drink from a glass during the ceremony. This is the time to learn how to achieve the four goals of the Apaches: physical strength, good disposition, prosperity, and a healthy old age.

It may take a year or longer to prepare for the ceremony. During the ritual itself, each honored girl wears a beautiful deerskin costume, a copy of that worn by White Painted Woman, the legendary mother of all the Apache. The costume includes an abalone-shell pendant strung across the forehead. Each girl has an older woman as her attendant and instructor. This is a very important role. Another major participant in the Sunrise Dance is the singer who leads the ritual chanting. He also guides the building of the sacred tepee, which represents the universe.

During this elaborate ceremony the girl receives many blessings, some brought each evening by cere-monial dancers who wear costumes and masks to represent the Mountain Spirits, spiritual beings who remain very sacred to the Apaches and live in certain mountains. She gives blessings as well, because she is said to have special powers at this time to heal the sick and bring rain to her people. Here is a marked

difference from those societies in which a female's powers at puberty are considered dangerous. Apache parents bring their children to the new woman for her blessings.

After the public festivities conclude, the ceremonial tepee is dismantled. Then each girl goes to a separate shelter for four days of private rituals. When the girls return home from this final initiation, they are considered women, ready for marriage.

Apache boys do not have as elaborate rituals for their own coming of age. However, their transition does not go unnoticed. It is marked by tests of their strength, skills, and basic physical endurance.

THE NAVAJOS · Among the Navajos, a girl's puberty is celebrated in *kinaaldá*, a four-day ritual performed to bring the girl good fortune, happiness, perfection, and fertility. Like other Navajo ceremonies, the kinaaldá is based on one of the Navajo song cycles. Each group of songs or chants offers blessings and tells stories from the Navajos' legends. The cycles are sung in Navajo healing ceremonies, which are performed to cure the sick and to restore harmony with the universe. The kinaaldá is based upon the song cycle called the Blessing Way.

Most of the ceremony is held in the girl's family home, known as a hogan. Songs are sung every day and night. During the fourth and last night, the hogan fills with the sounds of an all-night sing. As

DURING HER SUNRISE DANCE, AN APACHE GIRL IS SPRINKLED WITH A MIXTURE OF SACRED YELLOW CATTAIL POLLEN AND WATER.

the lead singer performs, his words transform the family's hogan into a holy place. Everyone who enters it becomes holy, too.

The first kinaaldá was held for Changing Woman, one of the most important heroines in Navajo tradition. Changing Woman is said to have brought people many things, including fertility and long life. She is responsible for molding each individual's personality and body. Her name comes from her ability to change from a baby to a girl to a woman and then back again at will. She is the ever-changing moon.

To honor Changing Woman and to become like her, the kinaaldá girl wears ceremonial clothes that resemble hers. These include many layers of finery and several special necklaces. The initiate ties her hair back in a loose thong as Changing Woman did. Once costumed, she receives a massage from several older, respected women. This "molding" is believed necessary because at this special time, the girl's body is said to be as soft as it was when she was first born. The ritual theme of rebirth is present here.

After her massage, the girl is ready to welcome guests into her house. She faces east, and lifts each guest's face upward. In this way she transfers to them some of the power she is believed to possess.

Then she leaves the hogan, to lead a run with other young people along a traditional path. The runners travel eastward from the hogan toward the sun, and return westward to the hogan. This is the girl's pursuit of the sun, whose golden rays represent life, truth, beauty, and all else that is good.

During the next three days, the girl will run

along her path several more times. She will also diligently grind corn for a huge, sweet corn cake, known as an *alkaan*. This work helps her become industrious at this time when her character is being molded as well as her body. Some scholars believe that the cake is a symbol for the sun. Fittingly, it is made of corn, the most sacred of all plants to the Navajos and one that Changing Woman is said to have brought her people.

On the fourth day of the ceremony some of the men dig a large pit in which they start a fire that burns throughout the day. After sundown, the girl and her women helpers add the necessary ingredients to the corn so that it can be made into a cake. Then they shape it and pour the mixture into the pit. The girl blesses it with ceremonial corn meal before it is covered with corn husks. The fire burns all night to bake the cake.

While the cake bakes, everyone involved in the ceremony stays up all night at the girl's hogan, singing and listening to sacred Blessing Way songs. The chief singer leads the performance, with the kina-aldá girl at his side. They face the doorway, through which the first rays of the sun will come at dawn.

The songs sung throughout the night identify the initiate with Changing Woman. One of the songs includes this verse:

> *With beauty before me, I am traveling,*
> *With my sacred power, I am traveling,*
> *With beauty behind me, I am traveling,*
> *With my sacred power, I am traveling,*
> *With beauty below me, I am traveling,*

A Navajo initiate has prepared this alkaan, or sacred corn cake, which she will offer to others after it has baked all night over a fire pit.

With my sacred power, I am traveling,
With beauty above me, I am traveling,
With my sacred power, I am traveling,
Now with long life,
Now with everlasting beauty, I live.
I am traveling,
With my sacred power, I am traveling.

The songs continue until the sun rises. Then the lead singer begins the Dawn Song cycle. During these songs, the girl's hair, jewelry, and other physical attributes that connect her to Changing Woman are washed in a symbolic act of cleansing. Then a final race is run while special songs are sung.

The participants say the proper blessings after the singing is finished. Then they head for the communal center. The cake is ready now, so it is uncovered and cut up. The initiate serves a piece to each person. However, she does not eat any of it herself. In this way, she displays her graciousness, service, and unselfishness, character traits that all Navajo women are encouraged to possess.

During the final steps of the ceremony, the girl's body is painted with white clay and she receives her last molding. Each of these steps in her coming-of-age ritual were first performed for the kinaaldá of Changing Woman, as told in the Blessing Way song cycle.

When the kinaaldá is over, the initiate is considered ready to marry and bear children. She is now respected as a woman. Even more important, she receives the respect given Changing Woman; her kinaaldá rite has made her and Changing Woman one and the same.

THE VISION QUEST • Perhaps the most widely recognized Native American ritual for boys is the solitary journey many take to find a lifelong helper and guide. In tribes from the Eastern Woodlands to the Plains to the Northwest Coast, many Native American boys continue to mark their puberty with the event known as a *vision quest*. During this solitary retreat a boy seeks his spiritual helper, or Guardian Spirit. This invisible spirit will protect and lead him for the rest of his life.

A boy cannot be a successful leader, hunter, warrior, craftsmen, or anything else without a Guardian Spirit. The Spirit teaches the boy skills, often the same as those of his father or another close male relative. Some boys also receive special gifts that benefit their entire group, such as the power to heal.

On the Northwest Coast, where the Guardian Spirits traditionally dominate everyday life, the Spirit takes on an animal form and teaches the youngsters both ceremonial and practical things. For instance, a fisherman's son might find his Guardian Spirit appear in the shape of a salmon or a cod who teaches him special songs and dances as well as how to use fishing equipment. A canoemaker's son might meet his Guardian Spirit in the shape of a woodpecker; a hunter's son might encounter a Guardian Spirit that takes on the form of a wolf.

As the boy matures, he can call on his Guardian Spirit whenever he feels the need, and it will help him gain new insights, skills, and personal traits, such as courage and perseverance. His Guardian Spirit can also help him keep in touch with the unseen spirit world around him.

The exact way in which vision quests are conducted varies among Native American groups, but all of these solitary events have certain elements in common. Before beginning the ritual, purification of mind and body is necessary—a dip in a lake or river, or a sweatbath, which takes place in a sweat lodge. This structure is often made of wood and covered with animal hides or blankets and mud. In the center is a firepit where water is poured on hot rocks to create steam. The steam causes the participants to sweat profusely, releasing body impurities. Purification is often a ritual in itself, complete with chants, prayers, and herbs.

The boy is instructed by a medicine person or a close male relative before going on his first vision quest. Then he leaves his camp behind and goes to an isolated place in the mountains, forest, or desert where he lives by his wits for a period of time. In some tribes the boy has to be naked. Most groups allow the youngster to make a fire, but not to eat or drink. His goal is to have a vision, and usually a long fast produces the state of mind that opens a questor to the vision he seeks.

However, should the solo traveler become too hungry, homesick, or scared to wait for his vision, he is allowed to head for home. Then he can try again the following year. If he brings back a vision, his family or a medicine person interprets it. The interpreter needs great insight to do this job well.

Among many tribes, the vision a boy sees at this time also marks the time to change his childhood name to a grown-up name signifying his vision. (A girl is generally expected to keep her birth name.)

Among several tribes, including the Nez Percé in northern Idaho and the Algonquin around the northern Great Lakes region, girls as well as boys can have visions of Guardian Spirits. However, girls usually are not required to seek these spirit helpers, because it is considered dangerous for a girl to go off on her own. Along the Pacific Northwest Coast, for instance, girls might be kidnapped if found alone. Therefore, Native American girls in that region are only allowed to receive a Guardian Spirit if it seeks them out while they are going about their everyday tasks at home.

Today, in many parts of the United States, as Native Americans renew their ties with their past, ceremonies either continue or are being revived. At the same time, non-Indians are becoming more interested in the Indian way of life with its love and respect for the land. This interest has prompted several organizations to make vision quests available to everyone, regardless of heritage, sex, or age. During these wilderness experiences, a group sets out under the leadership of one or more able guides. When they reach a designated place, each seeker goes off alone for a certain time period. The base camp is within everyone's walking distance, however, so that anyone who needs to can return ahead of time.[3]

The goal of the participants is to make peace with themselves, as well as to connect with a spirit helper. While this non-Indian version of a vision quest does not lead to participants becoming tribal members, it does help them gain spiritual insights. Regardless of age, it may even serve as a rite of passage to a new stage of life.

CHAPTER SIX

COMING-OF-AGE AMONG WORLD RELIGIONS

There are thousands of religions in the world, each with its own doctrines and beliefs that are instrumental in shaping the lives of its practitioners. Judaism is the oldest of the major religions. It has played an important role in the development of Western culture, as has Christianity, which is the main influence on Western society today. Other major religions in the world are Islam, Hinduism, Buddhism, Confucianism, Taoism, and Shinto. Each of them celebrates its own coming-of-age ritual, except for the second-largest religion in the world, Islam.

JEWISH BAR MITZVAH AND BAT MITZVAH · The Jewish religion is based on 613 commandments, of which the Ten Commandments are the most well known. The commandments are basically rules for daily living. Jewish people believe that all of these commandments are a gift from God.

The Jewish coming-of-age ritual is the second of the main life-cycle rituals for Jewish people. The first ritual takes place shortly after birth, at which time the baby is given a name. For girls, this happens in the synagogue, usually on the Saturday after their birth. For boys, it is performed eight days after birth and involves the physical rite of circumcision, in commemoration of the agreement God made with Abraham, the father of the Jewish people. According to the Old Testament, God promised Abraham that if he and his descendants obeyed God's laws, they would become a great nation.

In Judaism, boys reach legal adulthood at thirteen years of age and girls at twelve. This age-dependent celebration differs from the other initiations explored in this book, in which initiations take place for young people when they show physical signs of puberty.

A Jewish boy who comes of age is said to be a Bar Mitzvah; a "son (Bar) of the commandment (Mitzvah)." A Jewish girl is a Bat Mitzvah, or "daughter of the commandment." Bar Mitzvah and Bat Mitzvah have come to be the terms for the ceremonies as well as that of the celebrants.

At the time of a Bar or Bat Mitzvah, Jewish children are considered mature enough to be held accountable to all the commandments. Age thirteen is also when males can serve as part of a *minyan*. A minyan is a group of ten men, the minimum number of people required to hold a Jewish prayer service.

Over the centuries, a traditional coming-of-age ritual has developed, during which the Jewish boy shows his spiritual community how well he can perform his adult religious duties. He does this by blessing the sacred book of the Jews, the Torah, and giving his first public reading from it at the synagogue.

The Torah, meaning "the teaching," consists of the first five books of the Old Testament. It tells the story of how the world began, the human race developed, and God came to rescue the Jewish people from slavery in Egypt and give them the gift of His commandments and laws.

The Bar Mitzvah is the center of attention on his special day. For the first time in his life he blesses the day's reading and recites some of the Torah itself before the entire congregation. He also makes a speech about his Torah reading. In the United States, his reading and blessing are usually in Hebrew (the language in which the Torah is written), but his speech is in English.

When the speech-making first began, it served as a way for the boy to demonstrate to the Jewish scholars in his community how well he had grasped his study of the Talmud, a book filled with commentaries on the Torah. The scholars gathered at the boy's family home on Saturday afternoon, or *Shabbat*, the holiest day of the week. The speech often spurred lively discussions. Afterward, the Bar Mitzvah's mother served the men a home-cooked meal.

The Bat Mitzvah is a recent development. The first one was held for the daughter of a rabbi, or Jewish religious leader, in 1922. Today, many Jewish boys have a Bar Mitzvah, while only some Jewish girls have a Bat Mitzvah.

In the United States today, there are three main branches of Judaism: the Orthodox, who keep to the old ways and hold services almost entirely in

Hebrew; the Reform Jews, who use both Hebrew and English and try to adapt the ancient laws to make them relevant to today, and the Conservative, who generally follow a middle road.

In Reform Judaism, men and women are considered equal, and girls have their coming-of-age ceremony at age thirteen as boys do. The Conservative ceremony for girls might be held at age twelve or thirteen. Among the Orthodox, Bat Mitzvahs are not held at all, because prayer is believed to be a man's responsibility.

The rituals for a Bar/Bat Mitzvah vary from congregation to congregation, but some elements of it are the same throughout the United States. A child is expected to study for many years before the ceremony, learning the Hebrew language, as well as prayers and theology. As the Bar Mitzvah nears, preparation becomes intense. This may include community service, known as *tzedakah*, meaning "righteousness" or "charity."

The ceremony usually takes place on Shabbat during the month following the child's thirteenth birthday (or in some cases twelfth for girls). At many synagogues, the date for the ceremony is set more than a year in advance.

For the synagogue services, the child wears a prayer shawl and can expect his or her parents to perform part of the services. The rabbi will usually

A HASIDIC BOY CUTS A PIECE OF CHALLAH, SPECIAL HOLIDAY BREAD, DURING HIS BAR MITZVAH, THE DAY WHEN HE BECOMES A MAN.

talk to the Bar or Bat Mitzvah about the new responsibilities he or she will be expected to assume.

Today, in many parts of the world, the synagogue services are followed by a festive celebration. This can take many forms, limited only by expense, imagination, and personal choice. It can range from a hayride or luncheon to a formal affair, which might offer a catered buffet or a full-course gourmet dinner and perhaps entertainment by one or more bands. Some youngsters have one party for their friends and another for their adult relatives and their parents' adult friends.

Bar Mitzvah and Bat Mitzvah celebrants often receive many presents from their guests, who may have come from thousands of miles away to honor the initiate and his or her family. In return, guests may receive a souvenir of the occasion. But while the festivities may be elaborate, they are still basically religious in nature and lead to an individual's acceptance into Judaism as an adult who can now read from the Torah and share in the responsibilities of his or her religious community.

CHRISTIAN CONFIRMATION • The Christian religion is based on the teachings of Jesus Christ, who Christians believe is the long-awaited Messiah. Today there are over one and a half billion Christians, making it the most widespread religion in the world.

Christianity is divided into many faiths. After a split in the eleventh century, the churches in Greece, Russia, and other parts of eastern Europe and western Asia became recognized as the Eastern Orthodox Churches. The Church in Western Europe became known as the Roman Catholic Church. Later, following the Protestant Reformation in the sixteenth century, Western Christianity divided into several bodies. Today the largest number of Christians are Roman Catholics. Christianity also includes many major Protestant denominations, such as Baptists, Congregationalists, Episcopalians, Lutherans, Methodists, and Presbyterians.

The Christian coming-of-age rite is called *confirmation*. On this occasion an individual renews (or confirms) the promises made for him or her at baptism. Baptism is the ritual that celebrates a person's first entrance into the Christian faith. In the early days of the Church, confirmation and baptism were celebrated at the same time. The first Christians immersed a person in water for baptism. Today, baptism is celebrated by the priest pouring or sprinkling water on a person's head or the person being immersed one or more times into water.

Although some Christian groups only baptize individuals who are old enough to give a profession of faith, today many Christians are baptized as infants. They then receive confirmation during adolescence. Although their parents have arranged for their baptism, they make their own decision to be confirmed and become part of the Church. Both baptism and confirmation are considered sacraments, initiations into the life of Christ and the Church community.

Several Christian faiths hold the sacrament of confirmation, including the Episcopal and Roman Catholic churches. Roman Catholic adolescents commit to a period of religious preparation, during which they may be instructed by priests as well as by lay people in Church history, religious theory, and prayer. Confirmation students may also be asked to perform community service by helping out in their parish or church administrative community. They may choose to work in the church office, help to teach younger children's religious classes, decorate the church at Christmas and Easter, keep up the gym, or assist at the nursery school during Sunday services. In some churches, they must also participate in retreats and take written tests to be sure that their studies are progressing well.

When the day of confirmation arrives, the young Roman Catholic men and women may wear special gowns. Often, a bishop performs the ceremony, which is held during a special mass. The confirmation takes place after everyone present makes a profession of faith. Then each *confirmant* is called up to the bishop and introduced to him by the parish priest.

In many churches, each confirmant has a chosen sponsor—someone who is special to him or her and personifies Roman Catholic beliefs. The sponsor stands behind the confirmant with a hand on his or her shoulder to give added strength. Then each confirmant kneels, renews his or her vows, and takes a confirmation name. This is the name of a saint whom they especially admire. In the future they may call upon this saint when they feel a need for guidance or spiritual strength. This invisible helping hand bears a similarity to the spirit guide found during the Native American vision quest.

Then the bishop anoints the confirmant with holy oil, symbolic of sealing the confirmation. He then makes the sign of the cross, tells the confirmant he or she is confirmed and says, "Peace be with you." "And also with you," the confirmant replies. Afterward, the family may have a small party or dinner, and the confirmant may receive gifts. Like presents for Bar and Bat Mitzvahs, these may be religious or secular in nature.

HINDU UPANAYA · Hinduism, which began about 1500 B.C., is one of the most important religions in Asia and the third-largest religion in the world. Today, of the more than 700 million Hindus in the world, most live in India. There are about 20 million Hindus in Asian and African nations and 350,000 in North and South America.

The oldest Hindu writings are the *Vedas*; the most familiar of which is the *Rig-Veda*, a text containing hymns to the gods. According to the *Rig-Veda*, there are thirty-three gods, the most important being Brahma, the Mystical Creator.

Hinduism divides society into five castes or classes, which themselves are divided into hundreds of smaller groups. The highest castes are the *Brahmans*, who are considered the most learned. They are the priests and religious teachers (the word Brahman means "one with God"). Then come the *Ksatriyas*, the warriors and rulers. Third are the *Vaisyas*, the shopkeepers and merchants. Fourth are the *Sudras*, which include the *Andshudras*, or serfs. In the fifth caste are the *Panchamas*, or untouchables, who are considered outcasts. The first three castes consider themselves the Twice-Born. Boys from these castes are said to receive a second birth through initiation. Girls have no special ceremony when they come of age, although they do have rituals when they are pregnant and when they give birth.

The age of initiation, known as *upanaya* ("the beginning of wisdom"), varies according to caste. Traditionally, a Brahman boy is supposed to be about eight years old when he goes through the sa-

IN THIS HINDU CEREMONY, A YOUNG BOY UNDER A SILK CLOTH
AWAITS SPIRITUAL REBIRTH. AFTER THE CEREMONY, HE WILL BEGIN
TO STUDY THE SACRED WRITINGS OF HIS RELIGION.

cred ceremony, a Ksatriya is eleven, and a Vaisya is twelve.

The ancient writings permit the initiation to be postponed until a later age if the boy is not yet ready to perform the duties expected of him. In any case, the ceremony is required to take place before a young man can marry. From the time it is performed until his marriage, the initiate is supposed to refrain from sexual relations.

At the coming-of-age rite for a Brahman boy, he receives the seven sacred threads that he is supposed to wear for the rest of his life. Before the ceremony, the boy's *guru* (religious teacher) carefully instructs him. In India, where astrology is important, a day is chosen on which the stars will be lined up in a favorable position. The night before the ceremony, the boy is supposed to remain in silent meditation. Early the next morning, the ceremony gets under way. In India it is usually conducted by a guru in the courtyard of the boy's house.

The participants are surrounded by plants, such as banana or mango trees. (In the United States, rose bushes or another plant that the boy likes might be used instead.) This natural setting turns the family courtyard into an altar. The initiate stands in the middle of a square made by the plants. He wears a fancy paper crown and a long silk robe that make him look regal. Near him a cup of oil burns.

His father (or mother) takes the cup of oil and places his hand over the flame, then gently touches his son's head, heart, and right hand. This symbolizes the passing on of an eternal flame of knowledge and spiritual blessing. Then the initiate's father welcomes his son and announces that the young man is a prince. He promises him that he will receive many worldly goods.

But the boy rejects the offer, thus beginning the main part of the "sacred thread ceremony." He tells everyone that he is giving up wealth in order to follow his guru and lead a simple life filled with faith, knowledge, and poverty. The guru will instruct the boy in the sacred writings, chiefly the *Vedas*. In return, the boy will be expected to show great reverence to the guru, whose teachings will help him live a more spiritually rich life.

The ceremony continues as the initiate's father begs him to change his mind, but he remains steadfast. He removes his royal robe. Beneath it he is wearing a much plainer garment. Then he takes up a crude walking stick, known as a *danda*. This is usually presented to him by his father. With his stick in his hand, the boy is ready to let his guru be his guide.

Upon hearing of the boy's determined choice, the guru places seven strands of string over the boy's shoulder. The strings represent the powers of speech, memory, intelligence, forgiveness, steadfastness, prosperity, and good reputation. They are draped in a traditional manner over his right shoulder and attached to his left hip. In the old days, the strings were supposed to be worn both day and night, throughout the boy's life. Today, it is not unusual for a Brahman to remove the strings when he goes swimming or takes a shower.

The boy also receives two prayer songs, which are known as *mantras*. These are supposed to be repeated and meditated upon three times a day for the rest of his life. If the boy recites his mantras as directed, while holding the sacred thread, it is believed that he can achieve self-control and strength.

The first mantra offers worship to Lord Brahma. It is whispered into the boy's right ear, usually by a guru who can speak the Sanskrit language in which it was originally written. According to custom, the initiate writes the second mantra himself as a prayer for inner power.

At the end of the ceremony, the boy is blessed by the guru, and he receives gifts, or alms. The food he may accept now is the first he has eaten all day.

After his initiation, the boy is ready to begin his quest for wisdom. He may start this lifelong search by spending some time meditating in a dark room, or he may take a vow of silence for a period of time. Like the initiate's mantras, these are ways for him to achieve greater self-control.

Each year after the ceremony, the boy celebrates the anniversary of his rebirth. On this special day he asks forgiveness for any wrongdoings he has committed during the previous twelve months.

BUDDHIST SHINBYU · Buddhism is one of the main religions that grew out of Hinduism. Founded by Siddhartha Gautama, a prince born in Nepal, Buddhism began in India late in the sixth century B.C. Gautama became known as Gautama Buddha, which means "the Enlightened One" or "the Awakened One." The Buddha claimed that although people think they are fully conscious, much of their time is spent in a dreamlike state. Buddhism was a rebellion against certain aspects of Hinduism, such as its worship of many gods and its emphasis on the caste system. Today there are more than 300 million Buddhists in the world.

In Buddhism, people try to reach a state of perfect peace and happiness. This is known as *nir-*

vana, and is only attainable by becoming detached from all worldly possessions and desires. Among the Buddha's teachings are the Four Noble Truths. These are:

1. Nobody in this world reaches total satisfaction. Life consists of several kinds of suffering, ranging from that felt when someone cuts a finger to that felt upon realizing that something once thought permanent, such as marriage, is actually a temporary state.

2. People suffer because they thirst for pleasures and material things, which they think will bring them happiness.

3. Suffering will end once a person comes to terms with what he or she is doing wrong and stops doing it.

4. The way to conquer suffering is to follow the Buddha's path, known as the Eightfold Path.

Buddhism is divided into two great schools, the Theravadan and the Mahayanan. The Theravadans believe that people can reach an awakened state on their own. The Mahayanans believe that a person's life is linked to all others, and so everything one does affects everyone else. Mahayanan countries include Tibet, China, Korea, and Japan. (It is more common to find women Buddhist teachers in Mahayanan countries than in Theravadan countries.) The countries of Sri Lanka, Thailand, and Burma follow Theravadan Buddhism.

In many Buddhist countries, young teenage boys spend months or years in a monastery, a community where Buddhist monks live together. During their stay, the boys receive special education in the Buddha's teachings.

In Burma, a boy becomes a man at the age of twelve or fourteen when he is initiated into the Buddhist priesthood in the Shinbyu ceremony. In a manner much like that of the Hindu initiation ritual, the Buddhist boy acts out his rejection of worldly goods for a life of meditation. The ceremony is often held in July at the start of the holiest period of the Buddhist year, known as *Wa*. The boy may choose to remain in the monastery for his whole life or to stay only for a few weeks or months.

The boy begins the ceremony in handsome clothes. Then Buddhist monks, in plain yellow robes and with shaved heads and eyebrows, help the boy exchange his elegant clothes for a robe like theirs. The initiate's head and eyebrows are shaved and he is taken away to the monastery.

The next day the boy returns to visit his home, accompanied by the other monks. Like them, he carries a begging bowl. Buddhist monks are not permitted to take anything and can accept only what others put directly into their bowls. The boy also has a new Buddhist name that he will use during his stay in the monastery. His tasks while there are to study and serve the monks. They teach him that nirvana is not a birthright but a state of mind that can only be attained through following the Buddha's Eightfold Path.

The Eightfold Path, a tool to get a deep understanding of the first three Noble Truths, is also a

path to becoming a good human being. In that respect, it is similar to the Ten Commandments and the seven strings of the Hindu initiation. It consists of:

1. Correct understanding—grasping the Four Noble Truths

2. Correct thought—thinking kindly and clearly about all creatures

3. Correct speech—speaking kindly and truthfully

4. Correct action—helping others in a peaceful manner, without anticipating a reward

5. Correct work—earning a living at a job that does not harm others

6. Correct effort—working to solve problems and to eliminate unhealthy thoughts

7. Correct mindfulness—focusing completely on what you are doing, and being considerate of others

8. Correct concentration—striving to become one with each situation so that your mind awakens more

NOVICES OUTSIDE A BUDDHIST MONASTERY IN THAILAND.

Today, in the United States, Buddhist communities—often founded by Asian-American immigrants from China and Japan—have helped to spread the religion. Eastern teachers now live in the United States and train American-born teachers. Many cities have groups of Buddhists who meet together for talks, study groups, and meditation. There are also Buddhist monks who allow young boys to join them for short periods of time.

One such group is the Cambodian Buddhist Society Temple in Fresno, California. There, young men may join the seven monks in the modest temple for a temporary stay after going through a ceremony in which their heads and eyebrows are shaved clean and their souls blessed. The boys will be expected to rise at five each morning to pray, then eat a modest breakfast, and start studying the Buddhist manuscripts. They will have a break for lunch, which is the last meal until the next morning.

These are some of the coming-of-age ceremonies that continue to be practiced by major world religions today. All involve a period of intense study and are distinguished by having the initiate wear special clothes and perform specific tasks. Such religious rituals may be group or individual events. They are similar to several rituals explored earlier because they involve elders passing on information to the initiates. In tribal societies this is primarily done orally, while the organized religions generally have texts for initiates to read.

The major difference between religious rituals and other coming-of-age rituals is that they acknowledge a young person's change of status to only a segment of society—his or her religious peers. Yet, although these rites do not unite all adolescents of an entire country, they are extremely important to the fabric of our society. They offer large groups of young people the insights they need to help them become compassionate, wise, and ethical human beings.

CHAPTER SEVEN
INDUSTRIALIZED COUNTRIES TODAY

Aside from religious rites, there are few coming-of-age rituals in today's industrialized countries. Among the exceptions are Japan's celebration of Adults' Day and Latin America's *quinceaños*, or *fiesta de los quince años.*

QUINCEAÑOS · Hispanic families celebrate the quinceaños to reaffirm a fifteen-year-old daughter's commitment to her church and family as well as to her community. As a *quinceañera*, a young woman carries on an ancient tradition. The *quince*, as it is commonly called, is believed to have been performed in Latin America and the Caribbean for more than five hundred years. It reportedly grew out of the puberty rites practiced primarily by the Mayas and Aztecs, whose existence revolved around their gods, temples, and religious events. The quince was performed so that the community would find favor with the gods by helping its young people to take their rightful place as adults. These ancient rites were designed to separate the child from his or her mother, introduce the child to sacred traditions, and initiate him or her into a life of service to the community. Ceremonies varied from group to group, with the Mayan ceremony being the most elaborate.[1]

In ancient Mayan rituals, elders led all the young people of their village—girls *and* boys—to a special place outside of the village. Until then, the young people had been educated at home by their mothers.

Away from the village, they went through six months of instruction about their culture, their sexuality, and the responsibilities of marriage. When they returned home, usually with a procession heralding their arrival, they were welcomed as adults. At some point, the quince began to be held only for girls. It continues to be held primarily for girls, but in some places boys are again encouraged to have one, too.

Although the quince is not a sacrament, like a confirmation, it begins with a religious reaffirmation in the form of a mass. Afterward, the celebrant, with her girlfriends and their escorts (known as the *damas y chambelanes*) may have a festive celebration. It is customary for the quinceañera to receive feminine gifts, such as perfume and jewelry, to mark her new status as a young woman.

Like a Jewish Bat Mitzvah, the occasion may be observed in a variety of ways, ranging from a small family party to an elegant affair with hundreds of guests and entertainment that lasts all night long. The size of the affair may be determined by the financial and social position of the girl's family.

In some places, the expensive private quinceaños has been replaced by an annual special mass and reception for all the girls and boys who have turned fifteen in the parish. In Dallas, Texas, for instance, parish teams prepare young people for the quinceaños mass held by the bishop each year to honor all the fifteen-year-olds in his jurisdiction. Boys and girls of all ethnic backgrounds are encouraged to go through the preparation and be honored.

ADULTS' DAY · Perhaps the most nationwide rite of passage found in any modern industrialized country occurs in Japan. Yet this ceremony, known as Adults' Day, is held long after the onset of puberty. Adults' Day probably had its origin in *gempuku*, a Japanese coming-of-age ritual for boys somewhere between the ages of ten and sixteen that was commonly held until the late nineteenth century. The name gempuku, meaning "basic clothing," comes from the fact that some basic addition to the wardrobe was given at this time to indicate that the individual was now considered a bona fide member of society, able to participate in community and religious affairs and to marry.

The exact change in clothing depended upon the social class of the boy's family. Someone from a noble family was presented with a distinctive cap, while a boy from the lower classes was given a loincloth. Girls had a similar ceremony between the ages of twelve and sixteen, involving changes in hairstyle and clothing. This was most often known as *mogi*, or "putting on the skirt." In some parts of the country girls also began to blacken their teeth at this time, as another sign that they had reached a marriageable age.

The concept of a gempuku or mogi survives in some communities of modern Japan. But the formal coming-of-age ceremony in Japan survives on a much larger scale in Adults' Day, which is a national holiday held every January 15. This special event honors every young person who has turned twenty during the previous year. In Japan, twenty is the age at which an individual is considered legally mature and may vote.

On Adults' Day, the young people wear special clothes and attend a ceremony that is usually held at the government hall. Afterward, it is traditional for the celebrants to visit religious shrines. (Most Japanese are Shintoist, Buddhist, or Christian.) Relatives may give the young celebrants gifts of business suits and formal *kimonos*, which are Japanese robes worn mainly by women. However, regardless of the ceremony, the Japanese tend to consider individuals immature until they have married or begun a career.[2]

COMING-OF-AGE IN THE UNITED STATES · There is nothing like an Adults' Day in the United States. And the religious coming-of-age ceremonies held in this country, such as Bar Mitzvahs and confirmations, do not automatically transform a child into an adult in the eyes of society as a whole. A boy who performs flawlessly at his Bar Mitzvah cannot move out the next day, get a job, and marry the girl of his dreams. Nor can a girl who has been confirmed expect immediate acceptance as an adult by her family and her community. Furthermore, teachers of religious edu-

THESE TWENTY-YEAR-OLD JAPANESE WOMEN
AND MEN ARE DRESSED IN KIMONOS AND
BUSINESS SUITS TO CELEBRATE ADULTS' DAY.

cation report that religious rituals have lost their meaning for many of today's youngsters.

On a nonreligious level, the debutantes' ball, or "coming out party," held for young women from wealthy families can be considered a type of coming-of-age rite, since they welcome the young women into a particular segment of society. Sweet Sixteen parties, also held only for young women, are not restricted by class. But no matter how elaborate these events may be, they do not give a young woman adult status. They are but one of many milestones along the road from childhood to adulthood in industrialized countries today.

The extended period of rebellious and moody adolescence depicted in the American media differs greatly from the brief adolescence of many tribal cultures where a powerful rite of passage bridges the gap between childhood and adulthood in a matter of days or months. Rites of passage have come to be a combination of legal sanctions granted by society, events acknowledged by a particular culture, and rituals accepted by one's peers as meaningful. The age of majority, when a young person is no longer considered a minor, is set by each state. But the markers and peer-group rituals start long before the laws make maturity official.

Perhaps the process begins when a twelve-year-old must pay full price for movie tickets and can no longer order a "kid's" meal at a restaurant. At age sixteen, an individual can usually apply for a driver's license. But there are other legal changes of note. At this age an adolescent can also leave public school and work without being restricted by child labor laws. At eighteen, a person can vote, join the armed forces, or marry without parental consent. Child protection agencies also consider people at this age as legal adults, no longer under their parents' jurisdiction.

Yet in many ways an eighteen-year-old in the United States is still a minor, who must wait until age twenty-one to buy liquor (in most states), enter into financial contracts, and run for public office. Although none of these laws identify exactly when adulthood has been reached, they help to show how prolonged adolescence now is in the United States.

Perhaps, more than anything else, graduation ceremonies from elementary school, junior high or middle school, high school, and college are the closest young people in the United States come to widely accepted initiation rituals. Some sociologists, such as Kenneth Keniston, maintain that because schooling is extended so greatly, adolescence is followed by another period, known as "youth." In youth, young people receive limited responsibilities for their lives. For instance, they can move away from home and live in a dormitory on their university campus, but they are still supported financially by their parents and supervised by school officials.[3]

Despite these milestones along the way, United States society keeps adolescents at a crossroad for some time, lacking both the protection given to minors and the rights accorded adults. Adolescents are often left on their own to work out their conflicts with adults and at the same time to come to terms with their own physical, emotional, social, and intellectual growth. And, throughout this whole period of both turmoil and joy, there is neither the divulging of tribal secrets nor a single event that serves as an entrance into the world of adulthood.

Without any significant puberty rites, adolescents generally struggle on their own or with their peers to attain the new status they want. Some sociologists think that joining a gang is how an alarming number of today's adolescents, particularly inner-city males, come closest to participating in an initiation experience. Although gangs may offer a sense of identity to their members, they are often linked to drugs and crime and other violent behavior.

The 1990s have witnessed a dramatic surge in youth gang activity. Ten years ago, only ten cities had serious gang problems. Today youth gangs are active in 125 U.S. cities.[4] Gang members are primarily between the ages of thirteen and twenty-four, and they have become more violent than in the past. These groups appeal primarily to youngsters in neighborhoods beset by poverty, racial strife, broken families, and meager job prospects. But gangs form in middle-class areas as well.

Gangs are highly developed subcultures, with dress codes and colors. Members may have cigarette burns on their hands or knife cuts or tattoos on their bodies to signify courage. Some members wear rapper-style sunglasses and "cake cutter" combs with sharp metal teeth. Observers note that gang culture can be highly ceremonial, with initiation rites that require an aspiring member to steal a car, fight the gang's leaders, or participate in a drive-by shooting. The vast majority of gang members are male, although many gangs have female associates, and there are some all-female gangs.[5]

Some counselors fear that in the absence of coming-of-age rituals and respected elders to guide them, many youngsters grasp the most obvious, but certainly not the wisest, signs of adulthood. These range from gang membership to smoking, drinking, using drugs, roaring down the highway in a car, making sexual conquests, and defying authority at every turn. Perhaps it is fair to ask if coming-of-age rituals are events that young people really need.

One person who would answer yes is Robert Bly, the author of *Iron John*. In his book, which brought new interest in anthropology to a popular audience, Bly proposes that men in modern society have lost something very vital by not going through coming-of-age rituals. He says that boys in tribal societies can turn to respected elders to help them make the transition to their next life stage. They can depend upon these elders for guidance and for initiation into the secrets and history of their community. Even more basic, the elders bring the boys in touch with what Bly calls the "male spirit."[6]

Bly holds weekend male initiation retreats that are attended by hundreds of men. The initiates spend two days singing, dancing, beating on drums, and sharing personal stories about growing up. According to Bly, while these men may be successful in their careers, they still crave a clean break from their parents and an initiation into the world of men. The widespread appeal of Bly's message is intriguing.

According to Vincent Woodard, a student of African culture, formal rites of passage are becoming popular among teenage boys in the United States as a reaction to the pressures of gangs and drugs, which are too often associated with being a man. Inspired by Woodard's studies in Africa, his younger brother Cedrick Woodard, seventeen, and his cousin Brandon Hammond, sixteen, recently held their own coming-of-age ritual that combined West African and African-American culture and religion.[7]

At the 6 A.M. celebration, performed on Mount Lemmon in Tucson, Arizona, the teens recited tales from Yoruba, a West African religion, and from African-American folklore of the South. They had both a private and a public ceremony. The private ceremony was attended by only their male relatives, who told stories from their own lives. Brandon felt that they all became closer to each other by doing this. He was surprised to learn that many of his relatives had faced problems and decisions similar to those he now faces.

Later, at the public ceremony attended by friends and relatives of both sexes, Brandon and Cedrick read declarations of their manhood, which they had written beforehand. The speeches included a summary of their lives and their expectations for the future. Brandon adds that his speech was "a way of getting some things off my chest." The teens were dressed in traditional African costumes. As in many other ceremonies, this one concluded with a hearty meal.

According to Cedrick, "A lot of African-American males . . . confuse manhood with being feared [by society]." He considered the occasion to be both a transition and a rebirth. Brandon reports that at least one woman at the ceremony was so impressed by it that she asked him to help her organize one when her own son comes of age.

Brandon Hammond and Cedrick Woodward celebrate a rite of passage in Tucson, Arizona, 1993.

Nobody said growing up is easy. Adolescence around the world continues to be an exciting time of change and challenge during which there are major developmental tasks to be done. In the industrialized societies we are most familiar with, both young men and women must learn to accept bodily changes, achieve mature relations with both sexes, prepare for marriage and family life, and gain emotional independence from their parents. Besides all this, adolescents need to choose a career to pursue as well as a set of values and ethics by which to live. These are no small tasks. Whether society-sanctioned rituals would help young people achieve them is something for each reader to decide on his or her own.

GLOSSARY

Aborigine. The first known people to inhabit Australia.

Adults' Day. Coming-of-age rite held for all twenty-year-olds in Japan every January 15.

Alkaan. Sweet corn cake prepared as part of the Navajo kinaaldá ceremony for girls.

Bar or *Bat Mitzvah.* Both the celebration and the celebrant for the Jewish coming-of-age ritual, usually held at the age of thirteen for boys and twelve for girls.

Bull-roarer. Piece of wood on a string that is swung in circles to make sounds from the spirit world.

Changing Woman. Legendary Navajo heroine who brought people fertility and other gifts.

Choma. Voluntary first initiation for African !Kung males.

Churinga. Pieces of stone or wood sacred to several Aborigine groups.

Circumcision. Genital operation in which the foreskin of a male's penis is removed or the female's clitoris is cut off.

Clitoridectomy. Genital operation on females; also called circumcision.

Confirmant. Name for the initiate in a Christian confirmation.

Confirmation. Christian celebration of initiation into the life of the Church observed by many Roman Catholic and some Protestant faiths.

Corrobboree. Special festival held among Aborigines.

Dreamtime. Mythological past for Aborigines.

Elima. Coming-of-age ritual for Mbuti girls in the Ituri Forest of Zaire.

Engwura. Last part of Aborigine coming-of-age rituals.

Ertwa-kurka. Partially initiated Arunta Aborigine male.

Gempuku. Means "basic clothing"; Japanese coming-of-age ritual held in the past.

Hogan. Traditional Navajo home.

Kinaaldá. Navajo initiation for girls.

!Kung. Division of San people who live in northern Botswana and adjacent Namibia and Angola.

Mantra. Hindu prayer song.

Manyatta. Camp for Masai warriors and uncircumcised girls.

Masai. Group of pastoral, seminomadic Africans living on both sides of the Kenya-Tanzania border.

Mbuti. Also known as Pygmies; short-statured people living in the Ituri Forest of Zaire.

Môça Nova. "New Maiden" initiation ceremony for Tukuna females.

Mogi. Means "putting on the skirt"; Japanese coming-of-age ritual for girls that was held in the past.

Moran. Masai warrior.

Nirvana. State of perfect grace and happiness that a Buddhist tries to achieve.

Nkumba. Ceremony for Mbuti and central African village males in Ituri Forest of Zaire.

Noo. Evil spirits in Tukuna legends.

Parish. Group of churches under one administration.

Potlatch. Ceremony held by several Northwest Coast Native American tribes that honors important events in life, including naming, initiation, and marriage.

Quince. Shortened form of Quinceaños (see below).

Quinceaños (Fiesta de los Quince Años). Coming-of-age celebration for fifteen-year-old Hispanic girls (and sometimes boys).

Sacrament. Formal Christian rite.

San. Tribal group in Africa.

Shapuno. Large communual dwelling in which the Yano-mamos of the Amazon live.

Shinbyu. Buddhist coming-of-age ceremony.

Timbo. Poison used in Tukuna female initiations.

Tukuna. Native American tribe located in the Amazon and known for its elaborate coming-of-age ceremony for girls.

Uaricana. Huge hollow log that serves as an instrument during the Tukuna ceremony, Môça Nova.

Upanaya. Initiation ceremony for Hindus.

Urliara. Name for an adult Arunta.

Urucu. Body paint used in the Amazon.

Veda. The oldest and most revered Hindu writing.

Vision quest. Solitary spiritual journey that serves as a rite of passage among many Native American peoples.

Voreki. Female Tukuna initiate during her coming-of-age ceremony.

Yanomami. Native American tribe located in Brazil and Venezuela.

SOURCE NOTES

CHAPTER ONE
GROWING UP HUMAN

1. Rolf E. Muss, *Theories of Adolescence*, p. 109.
2. Daniel Goleman, "Theory Links Early Puberty to Childhood Stress," *New York Times*, July 30, 1991.
3. Alice Schlegel and Herbert Barry, "The Evolutionary Significance of Adolescent Initiation Ceremonies," p. 698.
4. Judy Brown, "Cross-Cultural Study of Female Initiation Rites," p. 849.
5. Schlegel and Barry, p. 705.
6. Alice Schlegel and Herbert Barry, "Adolescent Initiation Ceremonies: A Cross-Cultural Code," p. 199.
7. Alice Schlegel and Herbert Barry, "The Evolutionary Significance of Adolescence Initiation Ceremonies," p. 711.

CHAPTER TWO
COMING-OF-AGE IN THE AMAZON

1. Karen Liptak, *Endangered Peoples*.
2. Ettore Biocca, *Yanoáma: The Story of a Woman Abducted by Brazilian Indians*.

3. Napoleon Chagnon, *Yanomamo: The Fierce People.*
4. Bruce Lincoln, *Emerging From the Crysalis,* p. 63.
5. Harald Schultz, "Tukuna Maidens Come of Age," *The National Geographic Magazine,* November 1959, p. 639.
6. Lincoln, p. 127.
7. Lincoln, p. 67.

CHAPTER THREE
COMING-OF-AGE IN TRIBAL AFRICA

1. Colin M. Turnbull, *The Forest People.*
2. David S. Wilkie and Gilda A. Morelli, "Coming of Age in the Ituri," *Natural History,* October 1991, pp. 55–62.
3. Andrew Fedders, *Maasai.*
4. Melissa Llewelyn-Davis, "Women, Warriors, and Patriarchs in *Sexual Meanings: The Cultural Construction of Gender and Sexuality,* pp. 332–333.
5. Cheryl Bentsen, *Maasai Days.*

CHAPTER FOUR
AUSTRALIAN ABORIGINES

1. Edward Weyer, Jr., *Primitive People Today.*

CHAPTER FIVE
NATIVE AMERICAN COMING-OF-AGE RITUALS

1. Karen Liptak, *North American Indian Ceremonies.*
2. Robert Moss, "We Are All Related," *Parade Magazine,* October 11, 1992, p. 8.
3. Robert Greenway, "Managing the Wilderness Experience," *Circles on the Mountain: A Journal for Rites of Passage Guides,* Winter 1990–91, pp. 19–23.

CHAPTER SEVEN
INDUSTRIALIZED COUNTRIES TODAY

1. Angela Erevia, "Quince años: Celebrating a Tradition," *Catechist,* March 1989, p. 11.

2. Itaska et al, eds., *Kodansha Encyclopedia of Japan*, p. 5.
3. Hugh Klein, "Adolescence, Youth, and Young Adulthood: Rethinking Current Conceptualizations of Life Stage." *Youth and Society*, June 1990, p. 462.
4. Charles S. Clark, "Youth Gangs: The Issues." *CQ Researcher*, October 11, 1991, p. 755.
5. Clark, p. 767.
6. Robert Bly, *Iron John*.
7. Taylor, Chanda, "2 Teens Celebrating Manhood." *Tucson Citizen*, June 6, 1993, p. 6A.

BIBLIOGRAPHY

Bancroft, Anne. *The Buddhist World*. New York: Silver Burdett Company, 1984.

Benedict, Ruth. *Patterns of Culture*. New York: The New American Library, 1934.

Bentsen, Cheryl. *Maasai Days*. New York: Summit Books, 1989.

Biocca, Ettore. *Yanoáma: The Story of a Woman Abducted by Brazilian Indians*. London: George Allen & Unwin Ltd., 1969.

Bly, Robert. *Iron John*. New York: Vintage Books, Random House, 1990.

Cawte, John. *Medicine Is the Law*. Honolulu: The University of Hawaii Press, 1974.

Chagnon, Napoleon. *Yanomamo: The Fierce People*. New York: Holt, Rinehart & Winston, 1977.

Cheneviere, Alain. *Vanishing Tribes*. New York: A Dolphin Book, Doubleday & Company, 1987.

Coleman, James S. *The Adolescent Society*. New York: Free Press, 1961.

Coleman, James S., and Torsten Husen. *Becoming Adult in a Changing Society*. Paris: Organization For Economic Co-Operation And Development, 1983.

Conger, John Janeway. *Adolescence and Youth: Psychological Development in a Changing World*. New York: Harper & Row, 1977.

Coon, Carleton S. *The Hunting Peoples*. Boston: An Atlantic Press Book, Little, Brown and Company, 1971.

Domnitz, Meyer. *Judaism*. New York: The Bookwrite Press, 1986.

Eliade, Mircea. *Rites and Symbols of Initiation*. New York: Harper Torchbooks, Harper & Row, 1965.

Fedders, Andrew, and Cynthia Salvadori. *Maasai*. London: William Collins Sons & Co. Ltd., 1973.

Fried, Martha Nemes, and Morton H. Fried. *Transitions: Four Rituals in Eight Cultures*. Toronto: George J. McLeod Limited, 1980.

Hawes, J.M., and N.R. Hiner, eds. *American Childhood: A Research Guide and Historical Handbook*. Westport, Conn.: Greenwood Press, 1985.

Kaplan, Louise J. *Adolescence: The Farewell to Childhood*. New York: Simon and Schuster, 1984.

Kett, Joseph F. *Rites of Passage: Adolescence in America 1790 to the Present*. New York: Basic Books, Inc., 1977.

Lightfoot-Klein, Hanny. *Prisoners of Ritual: An Odyssey into Female Genital Circumcision in Africa*. Binghamton, N.Y.: Harrington Park Press, 1986.

Lincoln, Bruce. *Emerging from the Crysalis*. Cambridge, Mass. and London, England: The Harvard University Press, 1981.

Liptak, Karen. *Endangered Peoples*. New York: Franklin Watts, 1993.

Liptak, Karen. *North American Indian Ceremonies*. New York: Franklin Watts, 1991.

Mayle, Peter. *What's Happening To Me?* Secaucus, N.J.: Lyle Stuart, Inc., 1975.

McCoy, Kathy, and Charles Wibbelsman, M.D. *The New Teenage Book*, Los Angeles: Price Stern Sloan, 1987.

MacDougall, Trudie. *Beyond Dreamtime: The Life and Lore of the Aboriginal Australian.* New York: Coward, McCann & Geoghegan, Inc., 1978.

Mead, Margaret. *Coming of Age in Samoa.* New York: Mentor Books, 1949.

Mead, Margaret. *Growing Up in New Guinea.* New York: Mentor Books, 1953.

Muss, Rolfe. *Theories of Adolescence.* New York: Random House, 1975.

Niethammer, Carolyn. *Daughters of the Earth: The Lives and Legends of American Indian Women.* New York: Macmillan, 1977.

Parrinder, Geoffrey, ed. *World Religions From Ancient History to the Present.* New York: Facts On File, 1971.

Rice, E. Phillip. *The Adolescent.* Boston: Allyn & Bacon, 1975.

Ritchie, Jane, and James Ritchie. *Growing Up in Polynesia.* Sydney, Australia: George Allen & Unwin, 1979.

Schlegel, Alice, and Herbert Barry, *Adolescence: An Anthropological Inquiry.* New York: The Free Press, 1991.

Springhall, John. *Coming of Age: Adolescence in Britain 1860–1960.* London: Gill & MacMillan, 1986.

Turnbull, Colin M. *The Forest People.* New York: Simon and Schuster, 1961.

Van Gennep, Arnold. *The Rites of Passage.* Chicago: University of Chicago Press, 1960.

Walker, Alice. *Possessing the Secret of Joy.* New York: Harcourt Brace Jovanovich, 1992.

Ward, Hiley H., *My Friends' Beliefs: A Young Reader's Guide to World Religions.* New York: Walker and Co., 1988.

Weyer, Edward, Jr. *Primitive Peoples Today.* Garden City, N.Y.: Dolphin Books, 1961.

MAGAZINES AND NEWSPAPERS

Bakan, D. "Adolescence in America: From Idea to Social Fact." *Daedalus 100*, Fall 1971. pp. 979–996.

Brown, Judy. "Cross-Cultural Study of Female Initiation Rites." *American Anthropologist*, 65/4: pp. 837–853.

Demos, J., and V. Demos. "Adolescence in Historical Perspective." *Marriage and the Family*, 1969, pp. 632–638.
Erevia, Angela, "Quince años: Celebrating a Tradition." *Catechist*. March 1989, p. 11.
Klein, Hugh. "Adolescence, Youth, and Young Adulthood: Rethinking Current Conceptualizations of Life Stage." *Youth and Society*, June 1990, pp. 446–471.
Martos, Joseph. "Putting Some Spirit Back into Confirmation." *U.S. Catholic*, October 1990, pp. 30–31.
Quintero, Nita. "Coming of Age the Apache Way." *The National Geographic Magazine*, February 1980, pp. 262–271.
Schlegel, Alice, and Herbert Barry. "The Evolutionary Significance of Adolescent Initiation Ceremonies." *American Ethnologist*, 1980, pp. 696–715.
Schlegel, Alice, and Herbert Barry, "Adolescent Initiation Ceremonies: A Cross-Cultural Code." *Ethnology*, 1979, 18/2: pp. 199–220.
Schultz, Harald. "Tukuna Maidens Come of Age." *The National Geographic Magazine*, November 1959, pp. 629–649.
Starr, Jerold M. "American Youth in the 1980s." *Youth and Society*, June 1986, pp. 323–343.
Strickland, Charles E., and Andrew M. Ambrose. "The Changing Worlds of Children, 1945–1963." *American Childhood*, ed. by Joseph M. Hawes and N. Ray Higer. Westport, Conn.: Greenwood Press, 1985.
Taylor, Chanda. "2 Teens Celebrating Manhood." *Tucson Citizen*, June 6, 1993, p. 6A.
Wilkie, David S., and Gilda A. Morelli. "Coming of Age in the Ituri." *Natural History*, October 1991, pp. 55–62.
Wright, Belinda, and Stanley Breeden. "The First Australians." *The National Geographic Magazine*, February 1988, pp. 278–292.
Yellen, John E. "The Transformation of the Kalahari !Kung." *Scientific American*, April 1990, pp. 96–105.

INDEX

Drinking age, 15, 103
Driver's license, 15, 102

Eastern Orthodox
  Churches, 82
Eastern Woodland Indians,
  63
Efe, 43, *45*
Eightfold Path, 91, 93
Eland Dance, 38
Elima (Mbuti coming-of-
  age ritual), 41–44
Engwura (Aborigine
  coming-of-age ritual), 60
Episcopalians, 83
Ertwa-kurka (partially
  initiated Aborigine), 59–
  60
Eunoto (Masai warrior
  graduation ceremony), 52

Face painting, 38, 51
Fertility, 24, 26, 34
Firebrand, 31
Fire ordeal, 60
Food, sharing of, 19, 38
Four Noble Truths, 90, 91,
  93

Gangs, 104–105
Gempuku (Japanese
  coming-of-age ritual), 99
Graduation ceremonies, 103
Great Spirit, 63, 66
Guardian Spirit, 74, 76
Gurus (religious teachers),
  87, 88
Gw/i, 37

Haida Indians, 65
Hair cutting, 23
Hairdressing, 51
Hair plucking, 31–32
Hammond, Brandon, 106,
  107
Headdresses, 29–30
Hebrew language, 79, 80
Hinduism, 77, 85, *86*, 87–
  89
Hogan (Navajo home), 69–
  70
Hunting, 39–40

India, 87
Initiates (*see* Coming-of-age
  rituals)
Iron John (Bly), 105
Islam, 77
Isolation of initiate, 16–17,
  22, 26, 27, 37, 64, 66
Ituri Forest, 40, 46

Japan, 90
  coming-of-age ritual in,
  99–100, *101*
Jewish coming-of-age ritual,
  15, 77–80, *81*, 82
Judaism, 77–80, 82

Kalahari Desert, 35
Keniston, Kenneth, 103
Kenya, 18*n*, 47, 48
Kimonos (Japanese robes),
  100
Kinaaldá (Navajo coming-
  of-age ritual), 69–71, 72,
  73

Sacrament, 83
Sacred thread ceremony, 88
Samoa, 10
San, 35, 36, 37–40
Sanskrit language, 89
Scars, 17, 40
Seven Sacred Rites (Sioux
    Indians), 66
Shabano (Yanomami
    dwelling), 21
Shabbat, 79, 80
Shaman (medicine man), 31
Shaving head, 46, 48, 49,
    51, 52, 91
Shinbyu (Buddhist coming-
    of-age ritual), 89–91, 92,
    93–94
Shinto, 77, 100
Sioux Indians, 66
Songs, 42, 49, 56, 69–71,
    73
South Pacific island
    societies, 10
Sri Lanka, 90
Stress, puberty and, 12
Subincision, 59
Sudanic villagers, 41
Sudras (serfs), 85
Sunrise Ceremony, 67
Sunrise Dance, 67, 68
Sweat lodge, 75
Sweet Sixteen parties, 102
Symbolic death and rebirth,
    16, 70

Taboos, 38, 46, 65
Talmud, 79

Tanzania, 47
Taoism, 77
Tattoos, 17
Ten Commandments, 77
Tests of endurance and
    bravery, 18, 39–40, 46,
    60, 69
Thailand, 90
Theravadan Buddhism,
    90
Tibet, 90
Timbo (plant), 32
Tlingit Indians, 65
Torah, 79, 82
Tsimshian Indians, 65
Tukunas, 26–29, 30, 31–
    32, 33, 34, 37
Turnbull, Colin, 42, 46
Twice-Born, 85
Tzedakah (community
    service), 80

Uaricánas (musical
    instruments), 28
United States, coming-of-
    age in, 100, 102–106,
    107
Upanaya (Hindu coming-
    of-age ritual), 85, 86, 87–
    89
Urliara (adult Arunta), 60
Urucu dye, 29, 33

Vaisyas (shopkeepers and
    merchants), 85, 87
Valero, Helen, 23
Vedas, 85, 88

Venezuela, 21
Vision quest, 74–76, 84
Voreki (Tukuna initiate), 27–29
Voting, 15, 100, 103

Wakantanka (Great Spirit), 66
White Buffalo Calf Woman, 66
White Painted Woman, 67
Woodard, Cedrick, 106, 107

Woodard, Vincent, 105–106
World Health Organization, 18n

!XU, 37

Yanomamis, 21–24, 25, 26, 37
Yoruba, 106
Youth, 103

Zaire, 40